Back in the Days of Moses and Abraham: Old Testament Homilies for Children

Beverly Taylor

©1997 by Beverly Taylor
All rights reserved. No part of this publication may be reproduced or transmitted in any form or by any means, electronic or mechanical, including photocopy, recording or any information storage and retrieval system, without permission in writing from the publisher.

Living the Good News, Inc.
a division of The Morehouse Group
Editorial Offices
600 Grant Street, Suite 400
Denver, CO 80203

James R. Creasey, Publisher

Illustrations: Marcy Ramsey, Anne Kosel, Ansgar Holmberg, Betsy Johnson, Victoria Bergesen

Printed in the United States of America.

The scripture quotations used herein are from the Today's English Version — Second Edition, ©1992, American Bible Society. Used by permission.

ISBN 1-889108-17-0

Table of Contents

Introduction 5

Genesis 1:1–2:3 11

Genesis 2:4, 15-17, 25–3:7 13

Genesis 4:1-16 15

Genesis 6:1–9:17 17

Genesis 8:6-16; 9:8-16 19

Genesis 12:1-20 21

Genesis 15:1-6 23

Genesis 18:1-10a 25

Genesis 18:10b-14 27

Genesis 22:1-14 29

Genesis 25:27-34 31

Genesis 27:1-45 33

Genesis 32 35

Genesis 32:3-8; 33:1-20 37

Genesis 37:1-11 39

Genesis 37:1-11 41

Genesis 37:12-36 43

Genesis 39 45

Genesis 40:1–41:44 47

Genesis 42–45	51
Exodus 2:1-8	53
Exodus 3:1-15	55
Exodus 3:1-15	57
Exodus 4:1-17	59
Exodus 6:28–11:10	61
Exodus 12:1-28	64
Exodus 13:17-22	67
Exodus 13:17-22	69
Exodus 14:10-14, 21-25;15:20-21	71
Exodus 32:1-14	73
Numbers 11	75
Numbers 11:31-35	77
Numbers 22:1-40	79
Numbers 27:12-23	83
Deuteronomy 4:1-9	85
Deuteronomy 5:6-21	87
Joshua 4:1-24	89
Joshua 24:1-2a, 14-25	91
Judges 16:14-22	93
Ruth 1:1-17	95

Introduction

You invite them forward with a mixture of both joy and apprehension, these children of assorted sizes and ages. Adults shift to allow the escape from cramped pews and closely packed chairs. Small forms drop out into the aisles, then bob forward toward the front of the church, some holding hands, some looking back questioningly at parents. Many grin; others share your apprehension. They surround you, watching you closely, waiting for your smile, your touch, your greeting. You know you take a risk each time you welcome this unpredictable group forward, but you also know, as you settle together at the front of the church, that the next few minutes will be among the most rewarding of your week.

Each parish calls it something different: a children's message, perhaps, or a children's sermon or children's talk. Here we refer to it as a children's homily, a short presentation, based on a scripture story, that invites the children to enter into and experience the story of our faith. Each homily respects the children's own spiritual vitality, urging them to share their experience of God, themselves and each other in an environment of love and safety.

Why offer children their own homily?

Offering a children's homily says to the children: "This is a special time just for you, because *church is for you, too.* Here, in church, you are welcomed, delighted in, treasured, held in our arms as you are held in God's arms." A children's homily extends in a concrete way the embrace of our loving God to include these, God's most vulnerable children. "You are this important to us," is the message, as the children file forward to gather for their homily.

But a children's homily offers the children more than the important affirmation that church is their place, too. A well-prepared children's homily couches the basics of Christian experience in terms the children understand and own. It invites children to experience the truths of scripture from the inside out: Children don't learn *about* Jesus calming the storm, they imagine themselves, frightened and rain-soaked, clinging to the sides of the rocking boat, yearning for safety, holding their breath for the moment when Jesus says "Peace, be still," feeling the relief that Jesus brings to the storms they experience in day-to-day life. Children don't learn about the comfort of Jesus' hug, they exchange Jesus' hugs with each other, then take those hugs out into the congregation. You get the idea.

And the benefits of a children's homily go farther than the children themselves. If you regularly present children's homilies, you already know how often adults approach you after the service and say, "That was great. I got more out of your children's homily than the regular homily." A children's homily—perhaps *because* it presents its point so simply and clearly, with the added framework of childlike wonder and innocence—can profoundly impress and move. Never underestimate the power of a child's fresh perspective or sudden and unexpected insight.

Many of the adults watching from the pews don't have children, or have little regular contact with small children. The children's homily helps balance their lives with the wonder and delight the children take in these encounters with God and scripture.

In addition, when you present the children's homilies, you model for families, friends and relatives ways to engage the children they love in the journey of faith. Story-telling, movement, songs, games and the use of props and illustrations—all of these explore faith in simple ways that others can use as well. After a month or two of watching children's homilies, people begin to catch on, even unconsciously adopting the methods demonstrated in your children's homilies.

Who are these homilies for?

Back in the Days of Moses and Abraham: Old Testament Homilies for Children drawn from the first half of the Old Testament contains forty homilies, written for children from the age of four or five through eleven or twelve. Admittedly, this is a broad age range, and you may find some homilies seem more appropriate for the younger children than the older. We have attempted to provide something for all ages in each homily, including occasionally offering options within the homilies themselves. Keep in mind that a children's homily is not an instructional activity, and that age matters less when sharing in ritual and worship. In fact, a variety of responses can enrich the experience for all participants. You may want to invite older children to help younger children with certain tasks and responses. The older children will benefit from the sense of awe and wonder—the raw spirituality—of the younger children.

These homilies will work for both small and large groups, from less than half a dozen to as many as thirty or more. When appropriate, we suggest ways to change the homily for very small or very large groups; for example, in a large group, you may not be able to invite every child to offer a response to every question; do your best to let different children answer each question. In a small group, you may be able to reproduce a simple prop for each child to take home. For the most part, the size of the group will not matter, but if it does, you should be able to adapt each homily for the number of children you anticipate coming forward.

If you regularly have a larger group (more than twelve), consider recruiting another adult or teenage helper for each additional six or so children. This is particularly helpful when the homily includes more complex activities, or if another leader can provide a calming influence for restless children.

How do I prepare?

Each homily in this book includes:
- a scripture reference
- a quote from the reading
- a brief summary of both the reading and the homily
- a materials list
- directions for the homily
- a suggestion for closing prayer

We encourage you to begin your preparation by reading the scripture on which the homily is based. You might consider reading the story in two Bible versions, including *Today's English Version,* used in the preparation of these homilies. Think about the passage. You might ask yourself:
- What does this reading say to me?
- What truth about God, about others or about myself do I learn from this reading?

Then extend your question to include the children you anticipate will join you for the homily:
- What would I like the children to hear in this story?
- What does this reading say to them about the love and care of God?

After your own consideration of the reading, read through the summary of the reading and the homily, check the materials list and read once through the homily itself.

Most homilies in this book offer both an age-appropriate retelling of the scripture story and at least one activity to help the children enter into the meaning of the story (occasionally both story and activity are blended into one overall activity). Time limitations or personal preference may require that you use one or the other rather than both. Feel free to do so. The stories can stand alone; if you wish, a question or two taken from the activity may be enough to help you draw a story-only homily to a conclusion. Likewise, you may not wish to retell the story if it has just been read from the Bible or lectionary; in this case, simply follow the regular reading of scripture with the homily activity.

Once you decide how much of the homily you wish to present, gather your materials and practice telling the story. We encourage you to memorize the story, though you may certainly use your own words if you wish. Tell the story to yourself, a friend or a family member once or twice. Inexperienced at storytelling? Familiarize yourself with the two cardinal rules of storytelling—make eye contact with your listeners and make sure they can hear you!

At the conclusion of each homily we offer a prayer. Again, add to or adapt each prayer as you wish.

Some basic principles to keep in mind:
- *The younger the children, the shorter the homily.* One guideline suggests that children will sit still and listen one minute for each year of their age; for example, the average five-year-old will be there, attending to you, for five minutes, an eight-year-old for eight minutes. Keep that in mind at points in the homily when you are doing the talking, for example, during a non-participatory story. That's why these homilies incorporate lots of movement and interaction.

- *There are more people involved than you and the children.* The parishioners listen and participate along with the children. Face the parishioners as you sit down to present the homily. Speak loudly, slowly and clearly. Repeat answers given by children if the children speak too softly for the parishioners to hear. If you use a poster or another prop, make it big enough—and hold it up high enough—for the parishioners to see, too. If children participate in actions (other than in a circle or semi-circle facing inward), face them toward the parishioners. While you and the children are not performing for the parishioners, you do invite them to worship with you. Keep that in mind.

- *Respect what children say.* You don't need to correct the children, you need only allow them to experience the story for themselves, to find their own meaning and, if they wish, to articulate that meaning. God reveals God's self to children, as to adults, in the right ways at the right times. Trust God to do this in your children's homilies.

In the homily, affirm all children for their responses; a simple thank-you accomplishes this beautifully. You can also say, "Jared, you believe…" or "Deanna, you feel like..," reflecting back to children what they have shared. Acknowledge each child's right to believe and feel whatever he or she believes and feels without editorializing. At times you may be hoping the children suggest a specific idea; if they do not, simply suggest the idea yourself. Your ideas matter too, and the children want to hear them.

- *Expect the unexpected.* In these homilies you invite open responses from creative, uninhibited children. You cannot control what they say or do (nor would you want to). If they perceive you as a caring friend, they will want to tell you about their pets, toys, eating habits and other topics that you may prefer not to discuss when you are leading in front of your parishioners. This will happen. Expect it, flow with it and enjoy it. Welcome even off-the-wall comments with grace and good humor, but be cautious not to laugh at the children, even when the parishioners do. A child can easily feel hurt if a serious comment shared in trust is met with laughter. Show your respect for the children by responding appreciatively to whatever they say.

Deal with the unexpected comment by acknowledging the child and redirecting attention back to the story or activity. If a child continues, you can thank him or her for the desire to share and explain that now you would like to focus on the activity or story at hand. Ask the child, "May I listen to your story later, after church?" Be sure to follow through with the child later. You might also put your finger to you lips and say, "This is our quiet time, our time to listen to the story. Can you do that for us?"

It always helps to remember: The clearest message to the children does not come through the content of your homily, but through the loving relationship you offer them when you gather together.

On Sunday morning, make sure to bring your collected materials and this book. Take a few minutes for a final review. Place any needed materials unobtrusively near the area where you will gather the children.

We recommend that you gather at the front of the church. Children can sit in a semicircle around you on the floor. If the floor is not carpeted, consider purchasing a large square carpet remnant to make sitting more comfortable. Many churches have several low steps at the front of the church; you could sit on one of these or on a low stool. You could, of course, also sit with the children on the floor.

Once you and the children settle in, begin the homily. Look with love and respect at each young face before you. You are in for a treat: these children have invited you into a most sacred circle. Consider yourself honored …and see what God will do.

Dirk deVries
Senior Editor

Genesis 1:1–2:3

In the beginning...God created the universe. (Genesis 1:1, *Today's English Version*)

Summary

In this reading from the book of Genesis, God creates the world. In today's homily, children first experience the delight of creativity, then listen to the Genesis story retold.

Materials

Bible
a decorative gift bag in which you have placed:
- several small pieces of colored yarn
- modeling clay
- brass buttons or other small, shiny objects
- toothpicks or other small pieces of wood
- bright fabric scraps

Before the homily practice creating a simple yet imaginatively abstract "work of art" using the materials gathered in the gift bag. During the homily, you will use these materials to recreate your "work of art," thus illustrating for children the creative process. Read through the text of the homily to get a clearer idea of how your "work of art" could look.

Homily

Invite the children to come forward for today's homily and sit in a semi-circle in front of you.

Say to the children:
- Today I want to share something that I created during this past week.

Place the bag in front of you in view of all children. Slowly remove and assemble items as you explain what you are doing. The children will enjoy the mystery and surprise as you say, for example:
- On Monday, I created short little tufts of fibers from yarn, carefully deciding how to trim each piece. *(Demonstrate with several scraps of yarn.)*
- On Tuesday, I wondered how it might look if I put some clay and yarn together. *(Combine clay and yarn as the children watch.)* And then, on... *(Pause here, silently inviting children to respond with "Wednesday." If children don't respond, ask, "What day?")*
- Yes, on Wednesday, I decided to add some color to see just how colorful this might become. *(Place some bits of fabric, etc., onto the sculpture.)*
- On... *(wait for the children to supply the word* Thursday*)* Thursday I chose a shiny brass button to brighten my creation and some silvery foil to make it sparkle. *(Add button and foil.)* And on the next day—what day would that be?
- That's right, on Friday, I added this tall straight toothpick to give my

sculpture a point! *(Add toothpick.)*
- And then on… *(pause again and wait for children's response)* Saturday, I finished my creation with some wooden pieces that I put in here and here. *(Add wooden pieces.)*
- My work, my creation, was finished, just like this!
- Today is… *(pause again)* Sunday and I will sit and admire what I have made and share it with you, my friends. This is good. This is *very* good.

Discuss:
- What does it mean to create?
- What things have *we* created?
- Let's listen to a special Bible story about something that was created in a time so very long ago that we call it "the beginning."

Hold your Bible open to the book of Genesis as you tell today's story:

In the beginning, everything was dark.

God moved through the darkness, wondering. God wanted something more than just darkness. "I'll start with light," God said, "I will create light to brighten the darkness. Let there be light!" And it happened, just like God said.

For six days God kept creating, making the universe, making the world.

God said, "I have created the round orange sun to light the days and warm the earth.

"I have made the gentle glowing moon to shine at night, sometimes big and round and sometimes like a skinny slice of yellow melon.

"I have created the sky, the earth and all the stars that blink and twinkle. This makes me happy.

"I have made water where the fish can swim, trees where the birds can nest and high mountains where the wind can blow.

"I have made tall slender grass, sweet-smelling flowers, reaching for the sun, tiny insects that buzz and hum and huge, gray wrinkled elephants that splash and shower with their trunks."

And it was all very beautiful to God.

God said, "This makes me so happy. I love all my creation."

"But still," *(pause)*, **"I feel lonely. I want to talk with someone."**

So God created humankind…man and woman. God talked with God's new friends. God was pleased and said, "This is good."

On the seventh day, God sat back and admired the world, saying, "This is *very* good!"

Yes, in the beginning, God created. And it was very, very good.

Prayer
- Dear God, thank you for creation, for making our beautiful world. Thank you for creating us to be your children. *Amen.*

Thank the children for joining you and invite them to return to their seats.

Genesis 2:4, 15-17, 25–3:7

"You may eat of any tree in the garden, except the tree that gives knowledge of what is good and bad." (Genesis 2:16, *Today's English Version*)

Summary

In this reading from the book of Genesis, Adam and Eve disobey God and are expelled from the Garden of Eden. In today's homily, children first discuss how easily something unsafe can appear to be safe, then hear the story of Adam and Eve's choice of the "unsafe" tree of knowledge.

Materials

Bible
18" x 24" sheet of white tagboard
colored markers
scissors
two clear glass drinking glasses
plastic kitchen wrap
water
bottle of clear household ammonia

Before the homily prepare the following:
- Cut out of white tagboard a large, basic tree shape. Use markers to add details, color and a smiling face.
- Fill one clear glass with water and tightly cover the glass with plastic wrap. Fill the other glass with water and add a tablespoon of ammonia. Tightly cover this glass with plastic wrap too. **Note:** *Closely supervise these glasses—and the bottle of ammonia—before, during and after the homily!*

Homily

Invite the children to come forward for today's homily and sit in a semicircle in front of you.

Begin by discussing:
- Are there things we have been told we should not do, because they are not safe? *(Help children to consider unsafe activities like playing with knives or matches, etc.)*
- What do you think is in these two glasses?
- Do you think what is in these glasses is safe to drink?
- I know that one glass is safe to drink and the other is not. One glass has clean water, but the other glass has a cleaning solution that isn't safe to drink. They both look safe, don't they? You can't see the difference, but I *know* the difference because I put some of this *(hold up the bottle of ammonia)* in one glass. Even though it *looks* safe, if you drink it, it will hurt you and make you sick.

Let the children carefully smell the ammonia mixture. Continue:

- Today's Bible story is about Adam and Eve. God told them something was not safe to eat but they did not listen.
- Someone special is with me to tell this story—*Thelma Lee Tree.*

Hold up the tree prepared **before the homily**. Say:
- Hello, Thelma! *(Invite the children to greet Thelma as well.)*
- If we listen quietly, Thelma will tell us what she saw happen in the Garden of Eden.

Hold your Bible open to the book of Genesis as you tell today's story:

Hi, my name's Thelma Lee. I'm just one of the many old trees here in the Garden of Eden. I was here way back when Adam and Eve lived in the garden, at the beginning when God first made the world. Here we were, all *very happy* in the garden, enjoying everything God had created— when suddenly, things really changed!

Sometimes it's hard to tell a safe thing from a dangerous thing. I guess that's what happened to Adam and Eve.

You see, with all the trees in the garden that had beautiful fruit to eat, there was one tree that was not safe. God said, "You may eat of any of the trees in the garden, but not this one. This one is off-limits ...*not safe.*"

But when Adam and Eve saw how yummy that tree looked—I mean, that tree had the most *delicious* looking fruit I'd ever seen—round as the moon and as plump as a white marshmallow—well, they could not resist.

Adam said, "Eve, doesn't this tree look great?"

"Oh yes, Adam, it does." Eve reached up into the branches and snatched herself a round, juicy piece of fruit. "Here, Adam," Eve said. "I don't think it will hurt to try just a little piece."

I watched Adam and Eve that day ...that awful day that changed everything. God made Adam and Eve leave the garden of Eden and they never came back. I still miss them.

But God *had* said, "You may eat of *any* of the trees in the garden, but *not this one*." God was wiser and knew it was unsafe.

I wish Eve and Adam had listened to God...

If you wish, discuss:
- Who was trying to keep Adam and Eve safe?
- Who helps keep us safe?

Prayer

- Dear Heavenly Parent, thank you for giving us people in our lives to help keep us safe, people that help us know the difference between dangerous things and safe things. *Amen.*

Thank the children for joining you and invite them to return to their seats.

Genesis 4:1-16

The Lord was pleased with Abel and his offering, but he rejected Cain and his offering. (Genesis 4:4b-5a, *Today's English Version*)

Summary

In this reading from the book of Genesis, Cain, in jealousy, kills his brother Abel. In today's homily, children first compare anger to the filling of a balloon with too much air, then hear today's story.

Materials

Bible
4 balloons, all the same color
large paper bag
pin

Before the homily put a little air in one balloon; fill a second balloon about half full; fill a third balloon very full. Save the fourth balloon to inflate during the homily. Hide all four balloons in the large bag.

Homily

Invite the children to come forward for today's homily and sit in a semicircle in front of you.

Begin the homily with a riddle; say to the children:
- What are round, filled with air, enjoyed at birthday parties and often carried by clowns?
- That's right: *balloons!*

Open the bag and show children the three inflated (or partially inflated) balloons. Say:
- Here are three balloons.
- What's different about these three balloons?
- Which one do you think will pop more easily?
- What happens when we blow too much air into a balloon?
- Today's story is about two brothers. One reminds me of a balloon that's so full it could pop!

Hold your Bible open to the book of Genesis as you tell today's story:

Adam and Eve had two sons, Cain and Abel. These two brothers worked hard: Cain was a farmer who grew plants for food; Abel was a shepherd who raised sheep.

Cain and Abel both wanted to give God a gift. "What gifts can we bring to God?" Cain wondered. "Let's give God what we know best," said Abel. "I'll give God a sheep; you give God something from your farm."

Right away, Cain was jealous that Abel was a shepherd. Abel had many sheep—old sheep, young sheep, small and big sheep. "It will be easy for Abel to pick out a sheep to give to God," said Cain. "But I'll have to work hard to

harvest a gift for God from my fields. It's not fair." *(Blow some air into the fourth, uninflated balloon. Pinch it shut while you continue telling the story.)*

Abel went into his flock of sheep to find a gift for God. Cain grumbled as he headed into his fields. *(Blow more air into the balloon so it is partially inflated.)*

The more Cain thought about it, the angrier he became. It only took Abel ten minutes to find a gift for God; it took Cain three days. He said, "It isn't fair that Abel has it so easy." *(Blow more air into the balloon so that it is quite full.)*

When it came time to present their gifts to God, God accepted Abel's gift but not Cain's. This made Cain even angrier. *(Inflate the balloon to its fullest.)*

Cain said, "I will hurt Abel because God likes his gift best." And so he did. *(Use the pin to pop the balloon. Allow time for the children to settle down after the surprise of the balloon popping.)*

Say to the children:
- Like a balloon, Cain's anger and jealousy grew and grew. His anger started small, like this balloon… *(Show slightly inflated balloon.)*
- Then his anger grew… *(Show half-inflated balloon.)*
- And grew… *(Show fully inflated balloon.)*
- Until he lost control and hurt his brother… *Pow!*

If you wish, continue the discussion:
- When do we feel jealous or angry?
- What can we do with our anger, before it becomes so big that we *pop* and hurt someone?

Prayer

Thank you for reminding us about our feelings, God. Help us to know when we are angry and jealous. Help us to talk about our anger and jealousy before they get big. *Amen.*

Genesis 6:1–9:17

Rain fell on the earth for forty days and forty nights. (Genesis 7:12, *Today's English Version*)

Summary

In this reading from the book of Genesis, God saves Noah and his family in the ark. The children first participate in telling Noah's story by creating the sound of rain, then discuss what it means to listen to and obey God as Noah did.

Materials

Bible

Homily

Invite the children to come forward for today's homily and sit in a semicircle in front of you.

Hold your Bible open to the book of Genesis as you tell today's story:

God said, "Noah, I am not happy with what has happened to my world. I want to wash the world clean with a flood and start new."

"But God, what about my family and me? And what about the animals?" said Noah.

God said, "Noah, I'll save you and your family from the flood. And the animals, too! But first you'll have to build a great, big boat!"

Noah and his family started building the boat. His neighbors laughed and said, "We haven't had rain in months and months. Look at the sky! No clouds, just sunshine! Put away that hammer, you silly old man!"

The people made fun of Noah, but he didn't listen. Noah listened to God instead. He picked up his tools and did what God said to do.

"There! All finished!" said Noah. "What a handsome boat." Noah gathered his family and all the animals and loaded them into the boat. And then do you know what happened? Yes, it started to rain. Noah heard the rain start to fall on the roof of his big boat.

At first the rain sounded like this: *(Invite the children to rub the palms of their hands together, slowly at first, then gradually faster and faster, then slowing to a stop. Repeat.)*

Then the rain sounded like this: *(Invite children to place their hands in front of them like two ducks talking to each other. Ask them to begin tapping their fingers against their thumbs, gradually increasing the speed and then slowing to a stop. Repeat.)*

Now let's put these sounds together to make a rain shower. You choose how you want to make the sound of rain, either rubbing your hands or tapping your fingers. *(Do this together for several seconds.)*

If that's a rain shower, how might we create a rainstorm, a big, big rain? We could clap like this: *(Invite children to clap their hands, starting slowly and softly, then gradually clapping louder and faster, then slowing and softening their clapping until they stop.)*

I know another way to create the sound of a rainstorm; we can stamp our feet like this: *(Invite children to stamp their feet, slowly and softly at first, then gradually louder and faster, then slowing and softening their stamping until they stop.)*

What kind of rain did Noah and his family and the animals hear in the boat? Did they hear this? *(Rub hands.)* This? *(Tap fingers.)* This? *(Clap hands)* This? *(Stomp feet.)* It may have started like this *(rub hands)*, but I'm sure it ended up like this *(stomp feet)*. Together, let's create a Noah rainstorm. We can start off with soft rain and end with loud, splashing rain.

(Invite not only the children but all those in the church to join you in creating the sounds of rain, first rubbing hands, then tapping fingers, then clapping hands and finally stamping feet.)

(Stop the "storm" and say:) Noah trusted God even when others didn't believe. Noah obeyed God and built his big boat when God said it would rain. And my, oh my, did it rain! It rained and rained for forty days and forty nights.

Is that a long time? Yes, it is a long time. When it rains and rains for a long, long time the earth gets very wet and the water gets high. It rained so much during the time of Noah that the world flooded. That is a lot of rain.

But as Noah listened to the rain, he also kept listening to God. Noah trusted God. Noah obeyed God. And Noah, his family and all the animals waited, snug and safe inside the big boat, listening as the rain fell on the wooden roof above them.

If you wish, discuss:
- Why did Noah build the big boat?
- How did Noah listen to God? obey God?
- How can we listen to God? In what ways do we obey God?

Prayer
- Thank you, God, for giving us ears to hear the rain. Thank you for hearts like Noah's that hear and obey you, too. *Amen.*

Thank the children for joining you and invite them to return to their seats.

Genesis 8:6-16; 9:8-16

***"When the rainbow appears in the clouds, I will see it and remember…"** (Genesis 9:16a, Today's English Version)*

Summary
In today's reading from the book of Genesis, God promises never again to destroy the earth with a flood. In today's homily, children first discuss signs, then listen to the story of God's rainbow promise.

Materials
Bible
red tagboard
white tagboard
colored felt markers

Before the homily cut a stop-sign shape from red tagboard. Also cut out a rainbow from white tagboard and color it using red, yellow, blue, green, orange and purple markers.

Homily
Invite the children to come forward for today's homily and sit in a semicircle in front of you.

Begin the homily by showing children the red stop-sign shape prepared **before the homily**. Ask:
- What does this sign mean to us?
- Why is it good to remember what this sign means?
- Our church has signs, too. Let's look around:
  — Do you see a cross? The cross is a sign that reminds us how much God loves us.
  — Do you see candles? Candles remind us that Jesus is the light of the world.
  — Do you see water? The water of baptism is a sign of God's forgiveness and love.
- Listen while I tell you a story about Noah and a special sign from God.

Hold your Bible open to the book of Genesis as you tell today's story:

Back in the days of Noah there was a flood that covered the entire earth. This flood was so deep and so wet, it destroyed everything, everything except for Noah and his family, safe in the ark, in his great big boat. All the animals were safe in the ark, too. They were a little bit crowded, but they were safe.

After it had rained for forty days and forty nights, God said, "I will close the flood gates of the sky. This is enough water."

So God did that. And the flood water started to go down. *(Raise hand high, then lower, to show the lowering of the water.)*

The days of the flood ended and the ground became dry. Noah opened the door to the ark so everyone could go out. It felt good to see the earth, to touch the grass and feel the sunshine warm on their skin.

Ms. Noah said, "Look, I can plant a garden right over here and grow some vegetables." Noah stepped beside her, stretching his arms and smiling. "Yes, we can plant grain, too. It will be good! We will have a home again."

One of Noah's sons said, "Father, I am glad we listened to God and built the ark, but what if, what if…" *(Let your voice trail off.)*

"What if *what*?" said Noah.

"Well, Father," said the son, "what if we build our home, plant our seeds and get everything like it was before and then…" *(Let voice trail off again.)*

Right then, Ms. Noah spoke up and finished her son's sentence: "You mean, what if we do all that work and God decides to send another flood, right?"

"Yes," said the son, in a very worried voice.

God heard Noah and his family. God said, "I am putting a rainbow in the sky. It will be my sign to the world. When the rainbow appears, remember this promise to you and to all the animals that a flood will never again destroy the earth."

The Noah family looked up into the sky that evening, just about sunset, and there it was…a beautiful rainbow *(show the rainbow)*, a beautiful rainbow of red, blue and yellow with green, orange and purple, too.

"Look," they said, "there is the sign of God's promise."

If you wish, discuss:
- We have lots of signs in our world. Remember the stop sign? Remember the signs and symbols in our church?
- We have other signs, too. Who can show us the sign we use when we want to be very quiet? *(Place your index finger to your lips.)*
- Who can show us the sign we use when we want to listen? *(Cup hand behind ear.)*
- Who can show us a sign that says, "I love you?" *(Hug a child or two.)*
- Who can show us a sign that we love and worship God? *(Discuss and demonstrate kneeling, praying with hands together, etc.)*
- Let's use a sign right now as we say our closing prayer. *(Show children how to place hands together with fingers pointing upward.)*

Prayer
- God, we love the rainbow, the sign of your promise to Noah. Help us to remember your signs of love to us. *Amen.*

Thank the children for joining you and invite them to return to their seats.

■ ■ ■ ■ ■

Genesis 12:1-20

The Lord said to Abram, "Leave your country, your relatives, and your father's home, and go to a land that I am going to show you." (Genesis 12:1, *Today's English Version*)

Summary

In this reading from the book of Genesis, Abram, following God's call, leaves his home and travels to a new land. In today's homily, children first discuss the nature of altars, then hear the story of Abram's travels through Canaan.

Materials

Bible
10 smooth, flat stones or river rocks (5"-6" or larger)
large bag

Homily

Invite the children forward and sit in a semicircle in front of you.

Begin the homily by discussing:
■ What is an *altar*?
■ Yes, we worship God at an altar by saying special prayers, by kneeling, by celebrating the Eucharist (or communion).
■ Today's story is about a man who built altars.

Hold your Bible open to the book of Genesis as you tell today's story:

God said, "Abram, I want you to leave your country, your friends and your home. I want you to go to another place."

"Leave my country? my friends? my home?" That sounded scary to Abram. He thought and thought and finally said, "All right, God, I will go because I trust you."

And so Abram and his family packed their clothes, packed their food, packed their beds and blankets. They packed *everything*, and they moved, just like God said.

With goats, donkeys, cattle and tents, Abram and all his family walked and walked and walked until they came to a special tree in the land called Canaan. The tree was so special, it had a name: *Moreh*. It was a sacred, holy tree.

There, by the tree named Moreh, Abram said, "Here we will stop and camp."

God said, "I will give to you this land. It will be for you and your children, and for their children and for their children."

Abram wanted to thank God in a special way so he built an altar at Moreh. *(Lay two stones side by side on the floor in front of the*

21

children.) Abram prayed and worshiped God.

God said, "Abram, go and see more of the land I will give you."

So Abram and his family packed their clothes, packed their food, packed their beds and blankets. They packed *everything*. And then they moved.

They reached a place called Bethel and stopped. Abram wanted to thank God in a special way, so what do you think he did, just like at the tree called Moreh? *(Pause to see if children will suggest that Abram built another altar.)* That's right, Abram built an another altar. *(Lay another stone next to the first two so they are in a row.)* At the altar, Abram prayed.

Then God said, "Abram, go and see more of the land that I will give you."

So Abram and his family packed their clothes, packed their food, packed their beds and blankets. They packed *everything*. And then they moved.

Abram traveled from place to place. Each place where they would camp, Abram would build an altar. *(Lay one more stone, completing a base of four stones.)* All over Canaan Abram traveled and camped, traveled and camped, traveled and camped. Each time he stopped, he built another altar. *(Place two stones on top of the four that are your base.)*

When they reached one spot in Canaan, people said to Abram,

"You must leave. There is no food here. We are having a famine; it's dry and hot and no food will grow."

So… (pause for the children to join:) So Abram and his family packed their clothes, packed their food, packed their beds and blankets. They packed *everything*. And then they moved.

Abram said, "We will go back to Bethel where I built an altar before." And once again, on their way back, whenever they would stop to camp, Abram would remember God by building an altar. *(Place another stone.)*

Finally Abram and his family were happy to be back in Bethel. Abram wanted to thank God again, so what do you think he did? That's right, he built another altar. *(Place the final three stones.)*

If you wish, discuss:
- How did Abram say "thank-you" to God?
- In what ways do we say "thank-you" to God?

Prayer
- God, help us to remember to give thanks to you always. *Amen.*

Thank the children for joining you and invite them to return to their seats.

Genesis 15:1-6

"Look at the sky and try to count the stars; you will have as many descendants as that." (Genesis 15:5b, *Today's English Version*)

Summary

In today's reading from Genesis, God promises Abram as many descendants as there are stars in the sky. In today's homily, children explore the concept of *descendants*, then hear the story of God's promise to Abram.

Materials

Bible
1 very large tomato
sharp kitchen knife
black permanent marker
plate
napkin or paper towel

Before the homily, draw a face on a large tomato using a black permanent marker.

Homily

Invite the children to come forward for today's homily and sit in a semi-circle in front of you.

To begin the homily, ask:
- What is a *descendant?*

Invite a variety of responses from the children. Affirm all answers. Remember to repeat quieter answers so all parish members can hear.

Continue:
- To help us understand the word *descendant*, let's look at the descendants from a friend I brought along. His name is Max G. Tomato. Say hello to Max.
- Max said it would be okay to show you his insides.

Place the tomato on the plate and slice it in half, preserving Max's "face." Show the children both halves of the tomato and point out the mass of seeds. Remove the seeds with your finger or knife, keeping the outside of "Max" intact to preserve his "face." Hold the plate low enough so the children can see as you remove the seeds from the tomato.

Say:
- Do you think we might be able to count all of these seeds?
- Yes, possibly, if we took our time.
- What do you think would happen if we took just one of these seeds and planted it?
- Yes, it would grow into a tomato plant. And on that tomato plant, what might we find?
- More tomatoes! And those tomatoes would be descendants of Max G. Tomato!
- If each of these seeds grew into a tomato plant, we would have lots and lots of tomatoes. And those tomatoes would have lots of seeds that could grow more plants with more and more tomatoes, so many

tomatoes that we wouldn't be able to count them all!
- Just imagine, millions of tomatoes, all of them descendants of Max G. Tomato.

Put "Max" back together and show his face. Say:
- People are like my friend Max G. Tomato.
- You and I are all descendants of someone else.
- We are descendants of our parents, our grandparents, their parents and their grandparents.
- To be descendants means we all come from other people.
- Listen as I tell you the story of Abram and his descendants.

Hold your Bible open to the book of Genesis as you tell today's story:

One starry night, after dinner, while Abram stretched out on the floor of his tent, God came to talk to him.

Abram looked startled; his hands shook. God said, "Don't be afraid, Abram, it's me, your creator God."

Abram asked, his voice quivering, "Why are you here, God?"

"I have something important to tell you, Abram. I will be with you all of your life. I am going to keep you from danger and give you a great reward."

"A reward, God?" Abram said. "But why?"

"You are special to me, Abram. I will reward you with land that shall be for you and all your descendants."

Do we remember what the word descendants *means?*

Abram was puzzled. "But God, how can I have descendants when I don't even have one child? I am getting very old, Perhaps too old to have children at all!"

God said, "Walk outside with me." Together they went through the tent door into the black of the desert night. "Look at the sky and try to count the stars: you will have as many descendants at that. Trust me, Abram, just trust me."

Then God was gone.

Abram went back into his tent and laid down again. He thought to himself, God has promised that I will have a child, and my child will have children, and their children will have children, and their children will have children, and I will have many, many descendants —as many as the stars in the sky! I don't know how God will do this, but I will trust that God can.

If you wish, discuss:
- What does Abram trust that God can do?
- When do we trust God?

Prayer
- Dear Creator God, we remember your promise to Abram. Thank you for your promises to us. Help us learn to trust like Abram. *Amen*.

Thank the children for joining you and invite them to return to their seats.

Genesis 18:1-10a

"You have honored me by coming to my home, so let me serve you."
(Genesis 18:5b, Today's English Version)

Summary

In this reading from Genesis, Abraham shows hospitality to three weary travelers. In today's homily, children experience cool water, listen to background information about the story and then assist in reading a poem about Abraham and Sarah.

Materials

Bible
clear glass pitcher with water
large clear bowl
napkins or paper towels

Homily

Invite the children to come forward for today's homily and sit in a semicircle in front of you.

Invite children to play a pretend game. Explain:
- Let's all pretend that it is a hot, summer day. We are outside playing in the dirt. Our hands are getting very dirty as we play. *(Move your hands as if playing in the dirt.)* We keep playing and playing. Now our hands are *very* dirty, *very* dusty and *very* hot.
- What would make our hands feel cool and refreshed?
- Yes, it would feel good to wash the dirt and dust off our hot hands. Let's do just that. I will give each of you a napkin (or paper towel) to dry your hands. Then I'll pour some cool water over your fingertips so you can feel how good it would feel to wash our dirty, dusty, hot hands.

Place the bowl in each child's lap as you pour just a bit of water over his or her fingertips. Let each child dry his or her fingers with a napkin or paper towel. As you move from child to child, invite the children to talk about how the water feels. Once all have experienced the cool water, explain:
- I want to tell you a story from the Bible that happened a long time ago, long before there were cars, buses, trains or airplanes. To travel, people would either walk or ride on animals like horses or camels.
- Our story is about three travelers who were walking through a hot, dry desert. They wore sandals so their feet got very dusty and dirty and hot...just like we pretended our hands did.
- Because there weren't stores or motels, travelers would depend upon other people to give them a place to rest and food to eat.
- In our story, Sarah and her husband Abraham are generous and kind to some hot and tired travelers.
- I need your help to tell our story today. Here is your part; just wipe your forehead with the back of your hand as you say:
 — Whew, it's hot!

Practice this several times with the children, then say:
- ■ I'll motion to you when it's time to say your part of the story.
- ■ Listen closely and watch me so you'll know when it's your turn.

Hold your Bible open to the book of Genesis as you tell today's story:

Sometime just about noon or so
When the sun was heating the land,
Abraham went to the door of his tent,
And sat in the shaded sand.
The desert days were sweltering days
And he knew he needed his nap.
So he rested his head upon his hands,
With elbows propped in his lap.

(Indicate for children to say:)
"Whew, it's hot!"

Abraham sat in the door of his tent
And nodded half asleep.
His tired eyes drooped, he felt so pooped,
Too hot to utter a peep.
His peaceful time was suddenly broken,
He discovered he wasn't alone,
His eyes popped open, he shouted "hello!"
In his friendliest, welcoming tone.

(Indicate for children to say:)
"Whew, it's hot!"

"It's us! Three travelers! Right here!"
Now Abraham saw it was so,
"You look weary and tired, come rest
Share the shade of my tree, don't go."

Abraham stood, then went for the drinks
Sarah busied herself with the food.
Have some water! Here's some towels!
This certainly improved their mood.

(Indicate for children to say:)
"Whew, it's hot!"

The travelers did as Abraham said,
so happy to find a cool place.
Grateful for kind and generous folk,
each wiping the sweat from their face.
Shade and water! Food and drink!
Old Abraham knew what to do.
First one, then two, then three,
Washing feet, the best that he knew.

(Indicate for children to say:)
"Whew, it's hot!"

Sarah served by baking her bread,
And Abraham served in his way.
Needs of one, then two, then three
Were met on that hot, sweltering day.

If you wish, discuss:
- ■ What did Sarah and Abraham do to show kindness to the travelers?
- ■ How do you and your family show kindness when visitors come to *your* house?

Prayer
- ■ Dear God, help us to always show kindness to others as Abraham and Sarah did. *Amen.*

Thank the children for joining you and invite them to return to their seats.

Genesis 18:10b-14

"Is anything too hard for the
Lord?" (Genesis 18:14a,
Today's English Version)

Summary

In this reading from Genesis, God promises Abraham and Sarah that they will have a son. In today's homily, children discuss the meaning of names, then hear the story of the birth of Isaac.

Materials

Bible
a book of names that includes their meanings
self stick name tags
felt marker

Homily

Invite the children to come forward for today's homily and sit in a semi-circle in front of you.

Begin by asking each child, one at a time, to say aloud his or her name. Write each child's name on a name tag. Help children remove the backing from their name tags and to stick them on their shirts.

When all—including yourself—are wearing name tags, show the book of names and explain that the book not only lists many names, but also tells what the names mean. Look up a few of the children's names and read aloud their meanings.

Explain:
- Today's story is about Abraham and Sarah and the name they give to their baby boy.

Hold your Bible open to the book of Genesis as you tell today's story:

Abraham was a hundred years old, and Sarah was ninety years old. They were a lot like other people who lived back in their day: they had homes made of tents, they raised animals for food, and they traveled by foot on long desert journeys.

But Abraham and Sarah were different in two important ways: first, they trusted and worshiped the one true God, and second, they had never had any children, not one little girl, not one little boy.

One day, when Abraham rested in their tent, looking out through the door at the sky, Sarah sat down beside him.

"Abraham, what are you thinking about so hard? You have a far-away look in your eyes."

Abraham seemed not to hear, so Sarah spoke again. "Abraham, Abraham, what are you thinking?" She gently shook his arm with her hand.

"Oh, Sarah, sometimes I am so confused about God. God said that we would have a son, but look at us! We are old Sarah, too old to have children."

Just then, three visitors appeared by the tree outside the tent. Abraham and Sarah welcomed them and gave them something to eat. After they had eaten, the three visitors said, "We are messengers from God. We bring a message about your son."

"Well, what is it then?" said Abraham excitedly. "Tell us now! We're not getting any younger!"

The three visitors shared their good news: Sarah would have a son. And they promised to return in nine months to see the new baby and celebrate with Abraham and Sarah.

Sarah found it funny that the visitors thought she—a woman ninety years old—could have a baby. She felt like laughing, but not wanting to be rude, she excused herself and headed to the back of the tent. There she began chuckling to herself: "Ha, ha, ha. My goodness! Ho, ho, ho! I am *too* old and *too* worn out to have a baby." Then she really began to laugh, so tickled with the idea of an old woman having a baby that the three visitors overheard her.

When Sarah calmed down, she returned to the front of the tent. The visitors asked, "Were you laughing?" She lied: "I didn't laugh." But they all knew that she had. And she knew it, too.

Later, after the travelers left, Abraham said, "Sarah, I know that you laughed, but don't feel too badly about it. A few weeks ago, when God told me that we would have a son, I laughed, too. It does seem silly that God would give two old folks like us a son, but Sarah, I truly believe that God will follow through on this promise. Nothing is too hard for God."

Nine months later, Sarah had her baby. Abraham said, "What will we name this son, Sarah?"

They both knew a name was important. They finally chose a name. The proud parents named their son Isaac.

Discuss:
- What did Sarah and Abraham both do when God promised them a son?
- What do you think the name *Isaac* means?

Affirm all answers to this final question. If no child guesses correctly, explain that *Isaac* means *laughter*. Ask:
- Why did Sarah and Abraham name their little boy Isaac?

Prayer
- Thank you, God, for laughter and for names. We are glad that you kept your promise to Abraham and Sarah. *Amen.*

Thank the children for joining you and invite them to return to their seats.

Genesis 22:1-14

"Now I know that you honor and obey God, because you have not kept back your only son from him." (Genesis 22:12b, Today's English Version)

Summary

In the reading from the book of Genesis, God tests Abraham's love and faithfulness, asking for the sacrifice of his son Isaac. In today's homily, children first discuss hard choices, then listen to the Bible story.

Materials

Bible

Homily

Invite the children to come forward for today's homily and sit in a semi-circle in front of you.

Begin the homily by discussing:
- What does it mean to *choose?*
- To choose means to pick:
  — Shall I eat an apple or a banana?
  — Should I watch TV or play a game?
  — Will I wear my blue shirt or my yellow shirt?
- Sometimes choosing is hard, like when we have to pick between two really good things. Dad or Mom say, "Which would you like, ice cream or candy?" You like *both* ice cream and candy. Which would *you* pick?
- What other examples of hard choices can we think of?

As children suggest hard choices, invite them to say which they would choose in each case. If they are slow to suggest hard choices, you might use one or more of the following:
- going to a movie *or* visiting with grandparents
- going swimming *or* riding bikes
- eating a favorite food *or* getting to stay up late

Continue the discussion:
- Imagine that your dog has puppies, six cute, friendly, playful puppies. You name them all. You play with them every day. You love the puppies, each one of them.
- Then one day your mom or dad tells you that it's time to give the puppies away. You can keep only *one* puppy. How can you decide? You love them all!
- What a hard choice! How do you think you would feel if you had to choose just one puppy?
- In today's story, Abraham is asked to do something very, very hard. He has to make a hard choice.
- Let's see what choice Abraham makes.

Hold your Bible open to the book of Genesis as you tell today's story:

One day God came to Abraham and said, "Abraham, I want you to give me your son, your only son Isaac as a gift to me."

Abraham was shocked. He stammered, "But Lord, you gave us Isaac as a special gift. You promised Isaac to us many years ago when Sarah and I were old." Abraham felt afraid and confused.

God said again, "Abraham, I am the Lord your God. I keep my promises, but now I want Isaac returned to me."

Abraham did not understand. How could God make such a request? Abraham and Sarah loved their son, their *only* son Isaac. Isaac brought them joy. They played and worked together, and now God would take Isaac away? Not fair!

Abraham struggled to believe and trust God. God is God, but does God know best? Abraham would obey.

God said, "Take your son Isaac to the mountain and I will show you the place where I will come for your son."

Abraham hesitated, but he did as God asked. He gathered food, donkeys, servants and his son, his only son Isaac. When they reached the mountain God said, "This is the place, Abraham."

Together Abraham and Isaac went up the mountain. How do you think Abraham felt? Do you think he felt angry? hurt? scared? lonely? sad?

Abraham said, "God, this is so very hard. I am afraid, but I still trust you." Abraham prayed as they walked, assuring Isaac that God would provide for their needs.

When they reached the place where Abraham would offer Isaac to God, an angel came to Abraham and said, "Stop! God does not want to take Isaac. Now God knows that you trust and that you will obey. God knows you are willing to make the hardest choice of all, to lose your son, your only son Isaac."

I WILL BLESS YOU...
BECAUSE YOU HAVE OBEYED ME
GEN. 22

Prayer

■ God, thank you for teaching us about hard choices in this story. Thank you for being with us in all our hard choices, for giving us faith and helping us to trust that you know best. *Amen.*

Thank the children for joining you and invite them to return to their seats.

Genesis 25:27-34

He ate and drank and then got up and left. That was all Esau cared about his rights as the first-born son. (Genesis 25:34, *Today's English Version*)

Summary

In today's reading from Genesis, Esau sells his birthright for a bowl of soup. In today's homily, children first explore impatience, then listen to today's story.

Materials

Bible
large metal soup pot with a lid
large wooden spoon
water
red food coloring

Before the homily mix water and red food coloring in the pot.

Homily

Invite the children to come forward for today's homily. Ask them to sit in a semicircle around the pot. Explain that the pot will be used in today's Bible story.

Say to the children:
- Who knows what the word *patience* means?
- That's right, *patience* is waiting for something, even when you don't *want* to wait.
- Who knows what the word *impatience* means?
- That's right, *impatience* means not wanting to wait for something.
- Today's story is about two brothers. One brother is very impatient. Let's see what happens because of his impatience.

Hold your Bible open to the book of Genesis as you tell today's story:

Two older sons lived with their parents a long time ago. These two brothers were very different from each other.

"I like to hunt and fish and work in the fields," boasted Esau, the older son. His mom and dad called him their *first-born son*.

"I like to stay at home and do jobs around the house," explained Jacob. His mom and dad enjoyed Jacob's fine cooking.

One day, mother said to Jacob, "Why don't you cook some soup?"

"That's a good idea," Jacob said. He began making bean soup. *(Remove the lid and begin stirring the "soup.")* Jacob stirred the pot —'round and 'round and 'round. While he stirred he enjoyed the sound of the big spoon on the pot.

(Stir, tapping the spoon gently against the sides of the pot.) He enjoyed the smell drifting upward toward his nose. *(Lean over the pot and sniff.)* He enjoyed the red color of the soup. *(Lift some of the water onto the spoon for the children to see.)* "This is my best soup ever!"

Suddenly, Esau stood at the doorway of the kitchen, tired and hungry from his day in the field.

"Jacob, give me some of your soup!" he said gruffly.

"No, this soup isn't for you, Esau," said Jacob.

But Esau was very hungry and did not want to wait for the evening meal or take time to fix something himself.

"I want some soup, now!" he said impatiently and pounded his fist on the table nearby.

"What will you give me for a bowl of this delicious soup," said Jacob in a rather slow and thoughtful way. "What will you give me?"

Esau grew more impatient. He could hear his stomach growling. "I will give you one of my best hunting arrows."

"Noooo…I don't want that," said Jacob. "Give me something else."

"Well, how about my hunting knife. It's bright and shiny with a leather handle!"

"Oh, Esau, what would I do with that? No, it must be better than an arrow and better than a knife."

Esau was getting *very* impatient. *(Do you remember what that means?)* He wanted the soup, and he wanted it *now!* "Okay, Jacob, tell me what it is you really want, and I will give it to you. Just *hurry!*"

"You are mom and dad's first-born son. That gives you special rights that I don't have. Give me those rights, and I'll be happy to give you a bowl of soup," said Jacob with a sly look.

Jacob did not really believe Esau would give him his birthright, but he thought to himself, I might as well try. I'm tired of Esau being so impatient and bossy all the time.

Esau did not like waiting for things he really wanted, so he quickly said, "All right Jacob, it's yours! You can have my special place as the oldest, first-born son. Now, give me some soup!"

Jacob gave him a big bowl of bean soup and some fresh bread. When Esau finished he got up and left. Esau felt full for the moment and didn't even think about what he had done.

If you wish, discuss:
■ What did Esau lose because of his impatience?
■ When have we lost something because we were impatient?

Prayer

Dear God, teach us patience. Help us to learn to wait when we need to wait. *Amen.*

Genesis 27:1-45

"I gave him my final blessing just before you came, and so it is his forever." (Genesis 27:33b, *Today's English Version*)

Summary

In this reading from Genesis, Jacob tricks Isaac and steals Esau's blessing. In today's homily, children first watch a demonstration of a "sealed promise," then listen to today's story and receive a "surprise."

Materials

Bible
sealing wax with stamp
1 envelope
1 piece of 8-1/2" x 11" paper
marker

Before the homily make individual sealing wax pieces to give to each child at the conclusion of the homily.

Homily

Invite the children to come forward for today's homily and sit in a semi-circle in front of you.

Say to the children:
- I am going to make a promise to you right now: *I promise that after today's story I will give each of you something special.*

Write your promise in large letters on the paper as the children watch. Let them see the written promise, then fold the paper and place it in the envelope. Close the envelope and seal it using the sealing wax, explaining what you are doing as you do so.

Continue:
- Today's story is about a promise, a promise that someone made, a promise that could not be broken.

Hold your Bible open to the book of Genesis as you tell today's story:

Isaac had two sons, Esau and Jacob. Though brothers, Esau and Jacob were very different from each other.

Esau worked outdoors. His skin was rough and he had lots of hair. His voice was deep and gruff.

Jacob worked around the house. His arms had less hair. His voice was higher and quieter.

Like many brothers—especially brothers who are different—Jacob and Esau often quarreled.

Jacob did not like being the younger son. "Esau will get the blessing from our father because he is older," complained Jacob. "I want that blessing to be mine." So Jacob made a tricky plan: he would pretend to be Esau and steal Esau's blessing.

33

"Father, I have come for my blessing," said Jacob in a deep, pretend husky voice.

Isaac sat up in his bed and said, "Is that you Esau?"

Jacob lied and said, "Yes, father."

Isaac said, "But your voice sounds a little like Jacob, my younger son."

"No, father, I am Esau, your firstborn son." Jacob was glad his father was almost blind so he couldn't see his face turning red from the lie.

"Let me feel your arm. I know that your arms have much more hair than Jacob's," said Isaac.

Jacob was prepared. He lifted some animal fur onto his arm and said, "Here, father. Here is my arm. Feel how hairy it is and then you will know that I am truly Esau."

Isaac felt the arm and said, "What you say must be true. Come closer to me and kiss me on the cheek." Isaac sniffed to see if Jacob smelled like Esau, like animals and fields and sunshine.

Jacob was prepared. He had rubbed his clothes in dirt and on the animals so he would smell like Esau.

Finally convinced that Jacob was really Esau, Isaac blessed him, saying, "May your fields grow good food, may you lead our family and may no evil come to you."

Once Isaac said the blessing he could not change it. He sealed the blessing by his word. Do you remember how I sealed my promise in the envelope?

When Esau came in from hunting he went to his father's bed and said, "Bless me now father." Isaac began to tremble, realizing he had been tricked. Esau cried aloud, saying, "Bless me, too, father!"

But Isaac couldn't change the blessing. Jacob received the blessing and it had been sealed by Isaac's word.

Say to the children:
- Isaac's promise was sealed by his word, by speaking his promise, just like I used the sealing wax to seal my promise to you.
- What was my promise to you?

Open the envelope and read the promise you wrote. Hand out the pieces of sealing wax as you say:
- Here is the little surprise I promised each of you.
- Remember, this is not something to eat!
- Every time we look at our pieces of sealing wax, we can remember that Isaac kept his word and would not break his promise.

Prayer

Dear God, thank you for Isaac who kept his word. You keep your word to us too. You promised to love us...and you always do! Help us to keep our promises, too. *Amen.*

Genesis 32

"You have struggled with God and with men, and you have won; so your name will be Israel." (Genesis 32:28b, Today's English Version)

Summary

In this reading from the book of Genesis, Jacob wrestles with an angel and is given a new name. In today's homily, children first discuss dreams, then listen to today's story.

Materials

Bible
bed pillow
2 4" x 6" cards
marker
colored felt markers

Before the homily color one side of a card yellow and the reverse side of the card pink. Write the name *Jacob* on one side of the second card and *Israel* on the reverse side.

Homily

Invite the children to come forward for today's homily and sit in a semicircle in front of you.

Show the pillow and discuss:
■ What do I have here?
■ What does it remind you of? *(sleep, dreams, bed)*
■ Who of us dreams when we sleep?
■ Do we ever have bad or scary dreams? What's that like?
■ Today's story is about a man who *thought* he was having a bad dream but discovered differently.

Hold your Bible open to the book of Genesis as you tell the story:

Many years passed since Jacob had received his father's blessing. Now Jacob was returning to his homeland. Jacob worried that his brother Esau who lived there would still be angry. Esau had been very upset with Jacob because Jacob had tricked him and stolen his special rights as the older brother.

So Jacob said to his messengers, "Go ahead of me. Find Esau and tell him I am coming to see him."

"What if he does harm to us?" asked the messengers.

"Tell Esau I am sorry and want to come home," replied Jacob.

So the messengers set out ahead of Jacob to find Esau. When the messengers came back they said nervously, "We saw Esau! He is already on his way to meet you. He has four hundred men with him!"

This frightened Jacob. Jacob prayed, "God, you told me to go

back to my land and to my brother and family, so please protect me."

Then Jacob made a plan. First Jacob selected cattle, donkeys, sheep and goats to give as gifts to his brother. Jacob said to the servants, "Take these animals to Esau. Tell him they are gifts." So the servants left with the animals.

Then Jacob divided all his family into two groups. He sent half in one direction and he took the others in a different direction. When his group came to a river, Jacob said to them, "Go camp for the night over on the other side of the river. I will wait here for Esau."

In the night, Jacob's thoughts troubled him. During his restless sleep, a man suddenly woke him up! This startled Jacob. Am I dreaming? Or is this Esau, sneaking up to hurt me? "What do you want?" yelled Jacob. But the stranger did not speak. Instead, this stranger began to wrestle with Jacob.

The two wrestled and struggled and wrestled and struggled all through the dark night. One would grab an arm. Then the other would. One would grab a leg. Then the other would. One would be pinned to the ground. Then the other would be pinned to the ground.

As daylight peeked through the early morning clouds, the stranger said, "Okay, you win. I will go. Daylight is coming."

Jacob said, "You are not Esau, so who are you?"

The man replied, "I am an angel sent from God. I will give you a special blessing."

Puzzled by the stranger, Jacob ask, "What is the special blessing?"

"I will change your name. No longer will you be called *Jacob*, but from now on you shall be called *Israel*, because you have struggled with both God and with people." After speaking these words, the stranger disappeared.

As the eastern sky turned pink with morning light, Jacob sat alone, remembering and wondering. He sat for a very long time, until the pink sky turned bright yellow.

Jacob said aloud, "God changes the morning light from pink to yellow. *(Show pink side, then yellow side of card.)* And God changes my name from Jacob to Israel." *(Show Jacob side, then Israel side of card.)* Jacob stood, yawned, stretched a bit and then walked toward the river to find his family's camp.

Prayer

God, you have been the God of many people for a very long time, people like Jacob and his brother Esau and all their families. Thank you for being our God too. *Amen.*

Genesis 32:3-8; 33:1-20

"But Esau ran to meet him, threw his arms around him, and kissed him."
(Genesis 33:4a, *Today's English Version*)

Summary
In this reading from Genesis, Esau and Jacob, two estranged brothers, find reconciliation. In today's homily, children listen to today's story, then illustrate the importance of the words *I'm sorry* by mending a torn picture.

Materials
Bible
a large magazine picture of two people enjoying each other's company
cellophane tape

Homily
Invite the children to come forward for today's homily and sit in a semi-circle in front of you.

Discuss with the children:
- How many of us have brothers and sisters?
- What are our favorite things to do with our brothers and sisters?
- How many of us sometimes argue or fight with our brothers or sisters?
- Today's story is about two brothers who have been angry with each other for a long, long time.
- Let's see what happens to the brothers.

Hold your Bible open to the book of Genesis as you tell today's story:

Jacob moved far away from his home. He wanted to get away from his brother Esau, who was very, very angry with him.

Many years passed. Jacob married a woman named Rachel.

One day Jacob said to Rachel, "God wants us to move back to my hometown and be friends again with my brother Esau."

So Jacob and Rachel packed up all their tents, animals and supplies. Together they traveled toward Jacob's home.

"Rachel," said Jacob to his wife, "what if my brother won't forgive me?"

"God will help us and protect us," replied Rachel.

"But what if Esau's so mad he just wants to hurt me?" said Jacob.

"God will help us and protect us," replied Rachel again.

"But what if..." and so Jacob continued, asking Rachel all the "what if's."

Rachel answered him patiently each time, "God will help us and protect us."

37

As they reached his hometown, Jacob saw Esau running toward him. For a moment Jacob was afraid. Then he remembered once again what Rachel had said so many times to him: *God will help us and protect us.*

As Esau came closer, Jacob could see Esau's face. He looked happy.

"Jacob, my brother!" said Esau loudly. When Jacob heard this he ran toward Esau and they hugged each other. Because they were happy and because they were sorry for hurting one another, they cried.

"I'm sorry, Esau," said Jacob.

"I'm sorry too," said Esau. The brothers felt glad to be together once again.

Say to the children:
- What two special words did Esau and Jacob say to each other? *(I'm sorry.)*
- What do the words *I'm sorry* mean?
- When have we said the words *I'm sorry*?

- Here is a picture of two people, like Esau and Jacob. Do they look happy together?
- When they get angry, hurt each other and say bad things to each other, this is what happens: *(Tear the picture in two, splitting it between the two people.)*
- Now they are separated by their bad feelings and their hurtful words. Jacob and Esau were like this: *(Hold up the two halves).*

How did Esau and Jacob able to get back together? What special words did they use?
- This tape (show cellophane tape) is like the words *I'm sorry*.

Invite one or two children to help you tape the picture back together.
Continue:
- Saying "I'm sorry" helps bring people back together.

Hold up the mended picture for all to see.

Prayer

Dear God, thank you for teaching us to say "I'm sorry." We're glad we don't have to stay angry. *Amen.*

Genesis 37:1-11

"Joseph's brothers were jealous of him." (Genesis 37:11a, *Today's English Version*)

Summary

In this reading from the book of Genesis, the jealous anger of Joseph's brothers grows and grows. In today's homily, children first illustrate the consequences of unexpressed anger, then listen to today's story.

Materials

Bible
large building blocks (2 or more for each child)

Before the homily use the building blocks to practice building a tower that will topple.

Homily

Invite the children to come forward for today's homily and sit in a semi-circle in front of you.

Show children the building blocks and ask:
- What can we do with blocks?
- We can build things, can't we?

Give each child one or two building blocks. Invite children to place their blocks on top of each other. Allow the blocks to topple over when they get too high.

Explain:
- I think blocks are like the bad feelings we sometimes get inside.
- We all feel mad sometimes. *(Place one block.)* But if we get madder *(add several more blocks)* and madder *(add more blocks)* and even madder *(add more blocks)*, the anger builds up until... *(topple the tower by building it too high)* ...all our anger spills out and we say or do things that hurt people.
- Is that what happens in today's story? Let's listen and find out.

Hold your Bible open to the book of Genesis as you tell today's story:

Joseph was the baby in his family. He was the youngest son of Jacob, and, because he was born when Jacob was old, Jacob was very fond of Joseph and treated him extra nicely. How do you think that made Joseph's older brothers and sisters feel?

That's right, they became very jealous of Joseph. "That Joseph really makes me *mad*!" they'd say to each other.

Sometimes Joseph tattled: "Father, father, look what my sisters have done!" or "Father, father, my brothers are napping in the fields, not watching the sheep!" This made his sisters and brothers angry.

Then one day Jacob gave Joseph a special coat, more beautiful than

any coat given to Joseph's brothers and sisters. "Here, Joseph, I made this just for you," said Jacob. "It will remind all of us how special you are to this family, because you are the youngest." This made Joseph's brothers and sisters even *more* angry.

One day Joseph said to his brothers, "Listen, I had a dream! Do you want to hear about it?" The brothers listened for awhile, until Joseph said, "I think my dream means that someday I'll be like a king over all of you!"

"No way, Joseph!" the brothers said. They'd been mad before; now they were *furious*!

Then Joseph had another dream. "My brothers, listen to my dream. All of you will someday bow down to me. I will be your ruler and give you food."

Now the brothers were *enraged*. They went from upset, to mad, to angry, to furious and now enraged! Their feelings got bigger and bigger and *bigger*. *(Illustrate by again placing blocks on top of one another until they topple).*

The brothers and sisters said, "Someday we will hurt Joseph."

I wonder if they will?

If you wish, discuss:
- How many of us get angry from time to time?
- What happens when we let our anger grow and grow?
- How can we keep our anger from growing and growing?

Encourage children to consider the value of expressing their anger when they feel it, saying "I'm angry," and talking with adults about their angry feelings.

Prayer

God, thank you for this story of Joseph to remind us that we all get angry. Help us not to let the anger grow too big. Help us not to hurt anyone when we are angry. *Amen*.

Genesis 37:1-11

"He made a long robe with full sleeves for him." (Genesis 37:3b, *Today's English Version*)

Summary

In today's reading from the book of Genesis, Jacob makes a special coat for his son Joseph. In today's homily, children participate in retelling the story as they listen to "Joseph's coat."

Materials

Bible
child-size brown or beige coat
8 strips of colored material, 3-4" x 1-2':
  yellow, blue, orange, red, purple, green, white and black
8 safety pins

Homily

Invite the children to come forward for today's homily and sit in a semi-circle in front of you.

Begin the homily by asking:
- Who has a favorite coat or sweater?
- What is your favorite coat or sweater like?
- Today's story is about a father who gave his youngest son Joseph a very special coat. *(Select a child to wear the coat and to stand next to you during the story.)*
- Today we will pretend that this is Joseph's coat. We will pretend that Joseph's coat can talk. Can a coat really talk?
- Are you ready to pretend? Good, let's listen to Joseph's coat tell our story.

As you tell the story, pin each strip of colored cloth to the coat at the appropriate point in the story. As each strip is pinned to the coat, encourage the children to name the color aloud, inviting them to join in the refrain:
- *(Color)* is a good color.

Hold your Bible open to the book of Genesis as you tell today's story:

Hello, boys and girls. I am the coat of Joseph. I began as a plain coat like this *(point to coat)*, **but Jacob, Joseph's father, made me into a beautiful, colorful coat. Each color reminded Jacob of something special.**

First Jacob put... *(ask "What color?")* **...yellow on me** *(pin the color on the coat)*. **Jacob said, "Yellow reminds me of the sun. *God* created the sun to rule the day."**

Yellow is a good color.

Then Jacob put... *("What color?")* **...blue on me. Jacob said, "Blue makes me think about great oceans and bubbling waters. *God* gave water for the little fish and the big camels and for you too."**

Blue is a good color.

Next Jacob placed... *("What color?")* **...red on me. " Red looks**

like fire," he said. "We have fire to keep us warm when it's cold, and we have fire to cook our food."

Red is a good color.

How do I look? By this time I was really starting to like my job as Joseph's coat.

Then Jacob said, "Orange reminds me of sunsets. The sun dips like an orange ball and then suddenly splashes across the blue sky, before it disappears."

Orange is a good color.

Count my colors! *(Point to each as you say the number:)* One, two, three, four....four colors, and there are *more*!

The fifth color Jacob put on me was purple. He said it reminded him of the robes that kings and queens wear, and how important rulers are in the world. Then Jacob said,

Purple is a good color.

Next Jacob put green on me. He said, "God made all the plants many shades of green. The grass, the hillsides and the weeping willow trees."

Green is a good color.

Then Jacob found some special black that he placed right here.

He said, "God gives darkness as a time to sleep and rest from our work."

Black is a good color.

Finally, Jacob put white on me. Then Jacob said, "White will remind us that God gives us light to brighten the night and to allow us to see *all the colors*."

White is a good color.

Well, children, this was *just the beginning* of my coat. After the colors, Jacob added precious jewels and fabrics of all textures until I became the most beautiful, exquisite coat anyone had ever seen. People loved to admire me. *(Take the coat off the child and carefully place aside.)*

If you wish, discuss:
- What do colors remind you of? What does the color green remind you of? the color blue? white? black? yellow? red? orange? purple? *(Invite several responses for each color.)*
- Let's thank God for the colors we see every day.

Prayer

Thank you God for the beauty of your creation with all its many colors. *Amen*.

Genesis 37:12-36

Jacob tore his clothes in sorrow and put on sackcloth. He mourned for his son a long time. (Genesis 37:34, *Today's English Version*)

Summary

In this reading from the book of Genesis, Joseph's brothers sell him into slavery. In today's homily, dominoes illustrate the cumulative effect of hurtful actions. Children then participate in the telling of the story.

Materials

Bible
dominoes

Homily

Invite the children to come forward for today's homily and sit in a semicircle in front of you.

Arrange a line of standing dominoes (10-20) so that they will topple, each into the next. As you work, discuss:
- What are these?
- What makes dominoes fun to play with?

Children will likely mention the fun of lining up dominoes and letting them fall into each other, as they will guess you intend to do. When ready, continue:
- Let's see what happens when we tip over the first domino.

Ask a volunteer to push the first domino. Say:

- Now I want to tell you a story about some angry, jealous brothers.
- What they do reminds me of what happens when we push over our dominoes.

Hold your Bible open to the book of Genesis as you tell today's story:

Jacob told his oldest son Reuben, "Go to Shechem and care for our sheep."

Reuben said to his brothers, "Let's go; there's work to be done."

The brothers said, "But what about Joseph? What work will *he* do?"

Reuben replied, "Shechem is far away. Father will miss Joseph too much if he goes. Besides, Joseph is still young and we are older."

"That's not fair," one of the brothers said. "Joseph doesn't have to work as hard as we do."

The brothers were angry with Joseph. "Father likes Joseph *best*," they said. "Joseph gets special treatment."

Joseph stayed home while the brothers headed for Shechem to take care of the sheep. After many days, Jacob said to Joseph, "Go to

43

Shechem and check on your brothers."

Joseph hesitated. "But father, you know that my brothers do not like me very much. I don't want to go. I am afraid."

Jacob said, "I understand that you are afraid, but your brothers won't harm you." Joseph went because he loved his father Jacob.

When the angry brothers saw Joseph coming, they decided to hurt him.

"Wait," said Reuben, "I have a better idea. We won't harm Joseph, we'll just scare him! Put him down in a hole and leave him there!" Reuben said this because he had a plan; he would come back later and help Joseph out of the hole.

When Joseph arrived, the brothers grabbed him and tore off his coat. Joseph cried out, "Don't do this to me. I am your brother." But the angry brothers ignored Joseph's cries and threw him into a deep, dark hole!

When Reuben left to tend to the sheep, men on camels came by on their way to Egypt. One of the angry brothers said to the strangers, "Look, we can sell you a good slave." The brothers lifted Joseph from the hole and sold him to the strangers.

When Reuben returned and found that Joseph had been sold he cried aloud, "What am I going to do? What will I tell our father?"

What do you think the brothers will tell their father? *(Invite responses.)*

That night, around the campfire, one of the brothers said, "Let's take some blood from an animal and put it on Joseph's coat. Father will think that he was killed by an animal."

The brothers returned home and lied to their father. "Your youngest son, Joseph, has been killed by an animal. Look, we found his coat. It has blood on it."

What do you think Jacob did? How do you think he felt? *(Invite responses.)*

When Jacob heard the news he fell to the ground and began to cry. His sons—and all his daughters, too—could not make him feel better. He couldn't sleep. He wouldn't eat. All he could do was cry because he believed that his beloved son Joseph was dead.

Say to the children:
- How did the angry brothers hurt *Joseph? Reuben? Jacob?*
- Remember our dominoes? When we pushed one, the others all fell down. One wrong can hurt more than one person. One push eventually knocks down all the dominoes. One wrong—the brother's growing hatred of Joseph—eventually hurt the whole family.

Prayer

Dear God, thank you for reminding us that hurtful words and wrong actions, like falling dominoes, can go on to hurt many people. *Amen.*

Genesis 39

But the Lord was with Joseph and blessed him, so that the jailer was pleased with him. (Genesis 39:21, *Today's English Version*)

Summary

In today's reading from Genesis, Joseph trusts in God even when facing difficult situations. In today's homily, children first use spoons to illustrate degrees of "strength," then hear today's story.

Materials

Bible
2 flimsy plastic spoons
2 flimsy wooden spoons
2 sturdy metal spoons
small cooler with ice
pint of ice cream, frozen very solid

Homily

Invite the children to come forward for today's homily and sit in a semicircle in front of you.

Explain:
- I brought three kinds of spoons with me today: plastic, wooden, and metal. How do we use spoons?
- Although each of these is a spoon, they are not the same, are they? How are they different?
- What would happen if I tried to scoop hard, frozen ice cream with each of these different spoons?

Remove the ice cream from the cooler.

Demonstrate how a plastic spoon bends and breaks as you try to scoop the ice cream. Next use the wooden spoon, again allowing the spoon to break.

Then use the sturdy metal spoon, showing that although it is still difficult to scoop the hard, frozen ice cream, you can, with effort, get a good spoonful without the spoon bending or breaking.

Say to the children:
- Today's Bible story is about a man named Joseph.
- One of these spoons reminds me of Joseph.
- Listen to the story to see if you can tell which spoon. *(Hold up the three clean, unused spoons.)*

Hold your Bible open to the book of Genesis as you tell today's story:

Joseph was a young man when his brothers sold him as a slave. Travelers on their way to Egypt bought him. "Carry these heavy suitcases, Joseph," said the travelers. "We will ride the camels while you walk the whole way."

Joseph knew this wasn't fair, but he said, "I trust in the true God, and I will do my best, no matter what." God gave Joseph strength.

When they arrived in Egypt, the mean travelers decided they didn't need Joseph anymore. They sold him to someone else. "Here," said wealthy Potiphar to the travelers, "I will buy this man to be my slave and servant."

Joseph became the servant of Potiphar. He did all that he was told to do; he cleaned the house, cooked the food, worked in the fields and did all the laundry. It was hard work. Even though he did not like being a slave, Joseph remained strong. "I trust in the true God and will do my best, no matter what," said Joseph.

Potiphar soon liked Joseph a lot. He put Joseph in charge of everything in his house. "Look," said Potiphar, "thanks to Joseph, my crops grow tall, the house looks wonderful, and I don't have to worry about anything anymore!" Potiphar saw how Joseph trusted in God.

But one day, someone lied to Potiphar: "Joseph is not as nice as you think. He's doing bad things in your house."

Sadly, Potiphar believed the lies. He put Joseph in prison. Joseph, said, "This is not fair, but I trust in God and will do my best, no matter what."

Soon the boss of the prison saw Joseph's strength, too. He saw how Joseph trusted in God. The guard said, "Joseph, I see that you are a strong and faithful person. Please be my helper in the prison." So Joseph had a special place as a leader in the prison.

"I will keep trusting in the true God and doing my best, no matter what," said Joseph.

Say to the children:
- In today's story, Joseph faced three hard situations. Those hard situations remind me of hard, frozen ice cream. With each hard situation, Joseph trusted in God and stayed strong. Can we name Joseph's three hard situations?
  — First Joseph was sold to travelers who made him carry their bags. Joseph trusted in God; he didn't break in a hard situation.
  — Then Joseph was sold to Potiphar, who believed lies about Joseph. Joseph trusted in God; he didn't break in a hard situation.
  — Then Joseph ended up in prison. Joseph trusted in God; he didn't break in a hard situation.
- What spoon do you think Joseph is like? *(Show three spoons.)*

Prayer

Thank you for the story of Joseph, God, and for helping Joseph stay strong. Thank you for helping us to trust in you, too, even in hard times. *Amen.*

Genesis 40:1–41:44

The King removed from his finger the ring engraved with the royal seal and put it on Joseph's finger.
(Genesis 41:42a, *Today's English Version*)

Summary

In this reading from Genesis, Joseph is released from prison, interprets the king's dream and is made governor of Egypt. In today's homily the children discuss "saving" and help retell today's story.

Materials

Bible
piggy bank
handful of coins
colorful child's bathrobe, vest or jacket
gold necklace or chain
large ring
1 large sheet of yellow construction paper
scissors
paper clip

Before the homily use the pattern on page 49 to create a simple crown from a large sheet of yellow construction paper.

Homily

Invite the children to come forward for today's homily and sit in a semi-circle in front of you.

Begin the homily by showing children the piggy bank and asking:
- What is this? How do we use it?
- Yes, we use a bank to save our money. *(Invite children to drop the coins into the bank.)*
- Why do we put some of our money in a piggy bank? Why do we *save* some of our money?
- Today's story today is about a king who learns about saving.

Hold your Bible open to the book of Genesis as you tell today's story:

One day the king of Egypt had a strange dream. No one could tell him what the dream meant. Wise men tried, but they couldn't. Magicians tried, but they couldn't. The smartest people in all the country tried, but they couldn't. No one could interpret the king's dream.

Then one of the king's servants told the king about Joseph. The king sent for Joseph. He said, "My servant told me you can tell the meaning of dreams."

Joseph quickly replied, "No *I* can't, but *God* can reveal the meaning to you."

So the king told Joseph his dream:

I dreamed there were seven fat cows and seven skinny cows. The fat cows ate the skinny cows but it

didn't make them fat, they still were skinny.

Then I dreamed there were seven fat ears of corn on a corn stalk and seven skinny ears of corn. The fat corn ate the skinny corn, but the skinny corn still looked skinny.

"What a dream! What a dream! What can this possibly mean?" asked the king.

Joseph prayed to God, "Help me understand the dream."

"Well," said Joseph thoughtfully, "the dream is an important message to you from God."

The king was curious about Joseph's God, so he listened carefully.

"This is the meaning of your dream," said Joseph. The seven fat cows are seven good years of crops and food. The seven skinny cows are seven bad years when the crops won't grow. The seven fat ears of corn are seven good years and the seven skinny ears of corn are seven bad years when there won't be crops. The dream means there will be lots of food in your country for seven years and then for seven years there won't be food. The crops will fail. There will be a famine in all the land."

The king was worried. "What will I do?"

Joseph continued. "You need a wise person to help you rule the land so that you can save some food each year for seven years. Put some safely away for the seven bad years. Then you will have enough food so the people will not starve."

The king said, "I believe you are a man of God. I want you to take charge of the food in this country so that we will not go hungry."

That's how Joseph became an important ruler in the land of Egypt.

(Pause at this point in the story. Choose one child to play the part of Joseph *and one child the part of* the king. *Remember, girls as well as boys can take either of these parts! Place the paper crown on the head of* the king. *Ask* Joseph *to stand beside you.)*

Now back to our story:

The king gave Joseph a ring, a new robe and a beautiful gold chain to wear about his neck.

(Have the king *place these items on* Joseph.*)*

"Joseph," said the king, "now you will be in charge of all my food and all my money." *(Have* the king *hand the piggy bank to* Joseph.*)*

With the children, discuss:
■ How did Joseph help save the king and the people of Egypt?
■ How did God help Joseph help the king?

Prayer

Loving God, thank you for helping Joseph help the king of Egypt. *Amen.*

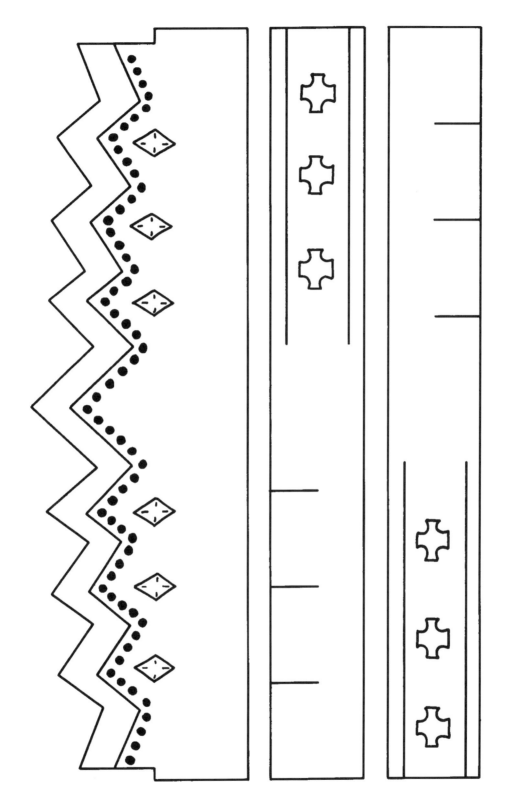

49

Genesis 42–45

Joseph told his brothers who he was.
(Genesis 45:1, *Today's English Version*)

Summary

In this reading, Joseph is reunited with his brothers and forgives them. In today's homily, children illustrate the slow healing of hurt feelings, then listen to today's story.

Materials

Bible
12" lengths of string or yarn, 1 per child
metal washers, 1 per child

Before the homily tie one end of each length of string to a metal washer.

Homily

Invite the children to come forward for today's homily and sit in a semi-circle in front of you.

Distribute a string and washer to each child. Explain:
- Hold up the end of your string high like this, so the washer hangs at the bottom. *(Demonstrate with your string and washer.)*
- With your other hand, give the washer a little push so it swings *gently* back and forth.
- Watch your washer go back and forth. Try holding your string until your washer stops swinging. *(Continue watching with the children until their washers have come to a stop.)*

As you wait for the washers to stop swinging, discuss:
- Has anyone here had their feelings hurt?
- Let's pretend that the washers swinging back and forth are our hurt, sad feelings. Sometimes it takes a long time for the hurt feelings to quiet down, become still and go away.

Collect the strings and set them aside. Say:
- Sad feelings and hurts don't go away immediately. The bigger the hurt, the longer it takes for it to go away.
- Today's Bible story is about a man who was hurt very badly by his angry brothers.

Hold your Bible open to the book of Genesis as you tell today's story:

Many years passed since Joseph's jealous, angry brothers had taken his coat and sold him as a slave. Now Joseph lived in Egypt. He ruled over all the food. Next to the king, Joseph was Egypt's most powerful ruler.

Joseph's angry brothers still lived in Canaan with Joseph's father, Jacob.

Jacob said to his sons, "There is a famine. Our crops will not grow. We need food. Go to Egypt; see if you can buy some food."

So Joseph's brothers traveled to Egypt.

When the brothers arrived in Egypt, Joseph recognized them. But they did *not* recognize Joseph. Joseph remembered how they had been so mean to him. Joseph thought, I won't tell them yet who I am.

Joseph asked, "Are you spies from another country?" The brothers said no. But Joseph insisted. "I think you *must* be spies from another country."

"No, no!" said the brothers. "We are honest, good men who only wish to buy food for our father Jacob, our little brother Benjamin and our families."

But Joseph put them in prison for three days. He still had some hurt feelings about all they had done to him. *(Hold up the string and washer and let the washer swing; pause for several seconds as the washer moves back and forth.)*

After three days, Joseph said, "Return home with this food, but if you want more food you must come back with Benjamin, your little brother."

Months passed. When Jacob and the brothers and all their families ran out of food, Jacob said, "Go back to Egypt and buy more food."

"We can't, father, because the ruler said we must bring Benjamin or he won't sell us any more food," said the brothers.

Jacob finally agreed to let Benjamin go with the older brothers to Egypt. Once more they traveled to Egypt.

Joseph sold them food but *still* did not tell them who he was. *(Pause as you allow the washer to swing again, this time only slightly.)*

Before they left, Joseph put his silver cup in Benjamin's bag of food.

After they left, Joseph sent his servants after the brothers saying, "One of you has stolen my silver cup." When the servants found it in Benjamin's bag they said, "Our master said whoever has the cup will have to die." The brothers were terrified; they had promised to bring Benjamin home safely to their father!

The brothers traveled back to Joseph. Then Joseph finally told the brothers who he was. *(Pause as you hold up the washer; allow it to slow to a stop.)*

"I am your brother, Joseph," he said. They all cried when they discovered that Joseph was alive. Though they had meant to harm him years ago, God protected Joseph.

Joseph said, "I forgive you." The brothers cried and were sorry.

If you wish, discuss:
- What is forgiveness?
- Forgiveness means letting go of hurt feelings, even when someone has said or done something mean.

Prayer

Heavenly Parent, thank you for forgiveness. Help us learn to let go of hurt feelings. *Amen.*

Exodus 2:1-8

The princess opened it and saw a baby boy. He was crying, and she felt sorry for him. (Exodus 2:6, *Today's English Version*)

Summary

In this reading from the book of Exodus, the king's daughter rescues baby Moses from the river. In today's homily, children participate in an active retelling of today's story.

Materials

Bible
basket
baby doll
blanket

Homily

Invite the children to come forward for today's homily and sit in a semicircle in front of you.

To begin today's homily, say:
- The Hebrews were slaves of the mighty king of Egypt. He did many mean, cruel things to the Hebrew people.
- This is a story about that time.

Hold your Bible open to the book of Exodus as you tell today's story:

One day the king's daughter said to her maids, "I am going down to the river to bathe. Please bring the soap and towels we need."

In those days the people didn't have bathtubs with faucets like we do, so the king's daughter and her maids went to the River Nile to take their baths. They laughed and talked as they moved through the tall bushes by the river.

When they reached the quiet pool area of the river, where the water swirled into a large circle, they set down their towels and soap.

"Quiet," said the king's daughter. "What is that sound?"

Everyone stood very still and listened closely. They heard nothing but the gurgling of the water as it flowed among the bushes. So the women began to talk and laugh again.

"Wait," said the king's daughter, "I hear it again."

"So do I," said one of the young women." *(Make a crying, whimpering sound.)*

But the noise suddenly stopped. So the women began to talk and laugh once more.

Then they heard it again. *(Make crying sound.)*

"What could it be?" said the king's daughter with a puzzled look.

She looked in the direction of the sound.

"There! *(Point to the basket.)* I see it. Look! A basket!"

Her handmaids brought the basket to her. *(Ask a child to bring the basket over to you.)*

Carefully, she pulled back a piece of cloth. *(Pull back the blanket.)* "Oh my," said the king's daughter. "It is a baby, a little frightened baby."

The baby began to cry. *(Make crying sounds.)*

The king's daughter recognized the child as a Hebrew child. Her father did not like Hebrew people and would be mean to the child.

She reached into the woven basket and picked up the baby, gently rocking him in her arms. *(Reach into the basket and take out the doll. Cradle it in your arms. Ask the children to pretend they each have a baby and to pretend to rock their babies.)*

Hold your baby and close your eyes; rock your baby quietly and gently as I tell you about this special moment when the king's daughter held the baby. Pretend you are the king's daughter. This is what you are thinking:

(Continue with a hushed voice:) "I've never seen such a beautiful baby. Look at the sunlight dancing across his tiny head. Who is this baby? Where is the mother? Harm will come to the baby because he is a Hebrew baby. I will rock the baby." *(Are you gently rocking your baby?)*

The handmaids silently watched as the king's daughter rocked the baby. Because the king's daughter felt love and compassion for the baby, she didn't want mean things to happen to the baby. She wanted to protect this beautiful, precious child.

"Please go find a Hebrew woman who can feed the baby for me," she said to one of her servants.

"I will keep this child and raise this child in the house of the king." As she rocked the baby she made up her mind that she would care for the child.

Discuss:
- How did the king's daughter show kindness and tenderness?
- When have we wanted to help someone who was hurting, lonely or sad?
- What can we do when we see someone who needs help?

Welcome many response to this final question. If necessary, give personal examples to help spark children's imaginations.

Prayer

Dear God, thanks for creating us to feel tender and loving toward those in need. Help make us aware of the needs of others. *Amen.*

Thank the children for joining you and invite them to return to their seats.

Exodus 3:1-15

There the angel of the Lord appeared to him as a flame coming from the middle of a bush. (Exodus 3:2a, *Today's English Version*)

Summary

In today's reading from the book of Exodus, God appears to Moses in the burning bush, calling Moses to be the leader of the Israelites. In today's homily, children first discuss what it takes to "get their attention," then listen to today's story.

Materials

Bible
large candle
holder for candle
box of matches

Homily

Invite the children to come forward for today's homily and sit in a semicircle in front of you.

Say to the children:
- When our parents want our attention, what do they say or do?
- At school, how does your teacher get your attention?
- How do fire fighters get our attention? police officers?
- What do *we* do to get someone's attention?

Without explanation, deliberately and very slowly strike the match and light the candle. Explain:
- I have your attention with this candle. All of you are watching me very closely.
- All of you are paying attention to me and what I am doing.
- Today's story is how God gets the attention of Moses.

Set the candle in a safe place during the telling of the homily.

Hold your Bible open to the book of Exodus as you tell today's story:

One day Jethro said to Moses, "Please take care of my sheep and the goats."

Moses said, "All right, I will care for your sheep and goats." Moses was happy to help Jethro. Jethro was the father of his wife, and Moses liked Jethro a lot.

"Thank you, Moses," said Jethro. "Please take my sheep and goats across the desert to the holy mountain called Sinai. There the grass is green and very thick. The sheep will like it."

So Moses packed all the supplies, said goodbye to his wife, gathered his servants and workers, and traveled across the desert with Jethro's sheep and goats.

When they reached the place by the mountain, Moses said to the

servants, "Let's set up our camp here. The sheep and goats will like this tall, thick grass. We will stay here for several weeks."

As the servants unpacked and set up the tents, Moses took a little walk away from the camp. He found a quiet place where he could be alone and rest. He shaded his eyes from the sun as it started to set in the west. Moses relaxed by listening to the birds, breathing the fresh air and resting with his own pleasant thoughts. Moses felt good.

Suddenly, the angel of the Lord appeared to Moses as a flame in a bush. Moses stepped back in surprise. What on earth is this? he thought. The flame stayed burning but the bush did not burn. The flame had his *total* attention.

"Oh," cried Moses. "Who are you and what do you want?"

The angel, who looked like a flame in the bush, spoke in a loud, firm voice. "Moses, you will be the leader of your people."

Say to the children:
- How did God get Moses' attention?
- In what ways does God get *our* attention?
- In what ways does God can get our attention here in church?

Hold the candle carefully as you say to the children:
- God used the flames of a burning bush to get Moses' attention.
- We use candles in our church. Candles help remind us of God's light and God's love.
- When we are reminded of God, God is getting our attention.

Prayer

Thank you, God, for the beauty of candles and for their light that reminds us of you. *Amen.*

Thank the children for joining you and invite them to return to their seats.

Exodus 3:1-15

"Now I am sending you to the king of Egypt so that you can lead my people out of this country." (Exodus 3:10, Today's English Version)

Summary

Today's reading from the book of Exodus tells of God's promise to help Moses be the leader of the Israelites. In today's homily, children first provide "missing information," then listen to and discuss today's story.

Materials

Bible

Homily

Invite the children to come forward for today's homily and sit in a semicircle in front of you.

Say to the children:
- You're going to have soup for lunch. You have the pot of soup and your spoon, what else might you need? *(bowl)*
- You have to go out in the rain. You have a raincoat and rubber boots. What else might you need? *(umbrella)*
- You want to make a picture for Mom or Dad. You have pencils, crayons and paint. What else might you need? *(paper, but allow a variety of answers)*
- In each case, something is missing, isn't it? We needed a bowl to eat our soup, an umbrella to stay dry in the rain and paper to complete a picture.
- Today's Bible story is about God needing one more thing to complete God's plan.
- God had a plan to rescue God's people from a cruel king, but God needed *one more thing*. God needed a *leader* for God's people.

Hold your Bible open to the book of Exodus as you tell today's story:

God said, "Moses, I want you to be the leader of my people. I want you to go to Egypt and help them get away from the mean, cruel king."

Moses was surprised. Moses was shocked. Moses was scared. Moses didn't think he could be the leader.

"God, I am nobody. How can I be the leader?"

Without explanation, set aside your Bible and begin moving your arms and hands into different positions, pausing each time so the children can follow and copy you:
- Raise your left hand high.
- Lower your left hand.
- Raise your right hand high.
- Lower your right hand.

Continuing silently, make different motions for the children to copy, long enough for all to catch on to follow-

ing, which they will. Say to the children:
- Have you ever been a leader? *(Suggest "line leader at school" or the "leader for a game" if children have difficulty remembering.)*
- What do you do when you are the leader? *(A leader helps us know things, like when we should move, where we should go, what comes next.)*
- How does it feel being the leader? *(Allow all responses, including feeling afraid, worried or scared.)*

Pick up your Bible and continue with the story:

Moses felt afraid. Moses continued telling God that he couldn't be the leader.

"What if no one will listen to me?"

God said, "They will listen, Moses."

"What if they make fun of me?"

God said, "They will respect you, Moses."

"But God," stammered Moses, "what should I say to all the people? What if no one believes that you asked me to be the leader?" Moses had many questions for God.

God said, "Say to the people, 'The God of Abraham, Isaac and Jacob sees your bad situation in Egypt. God will lead you to a different land.'" God wanted Moses to be the leader, and gave Moses much encouragement.

Moses continued asking questions and God continued encouraging saying, "I will be with you, Moses. I will help you know what to say."

Prayer

Thank you, God, for listening when we are afraid. Help us when we have to be leaders and do hard things. Thank you for the story of Moses that encourages us. *Amen.*

Thank the children for joining you and invite them to return to their seats.

Exodus 4:1-17

"Do this to prove to the Israelites that the Lord, the God of their ancestors, the God of Abraham, Isaac, and Jacob, has appeared to you." (Exodus 4:5, Today's English Version)

Summary

In this reading from the book of Exodus, God equips Moses to be the leader of the Israelites. In today's homily, children hear a creative retelling of today's story.

Materials

Bible

Homily

Invite the children to come forward for today's homily and sit in a semicircle in front of you.

Say to the children:
- What does it mean to *forget*?
- Have *we* ever forgotten something?
- Today we hear a story about Moses and his wife Zipporah. This story is about remembering something that was forgotten.

Hold your Bible open to the book of Exodus as you tell today's story:

One day, as Zipporah and Moses finished eating their lunch, Moses turned to his wife and said, "I don't think the Hebrew people will listen to me. I'm not a good speaker!"

Zipporah tried to assure Moses: "I think the people *will* listen to you."

Moses didn't think so.

"I wish I could help you," said Zipporah.

Moses stopped and thought for a moment. "Perhaps you can. Make me a new coat. The people will listen if I have a bright shiny coat."

So Zipporah made Moses a coat of purest white with big shiny buttons. It was the finest coat she had ever made.

"Here's your new coat. Now do you think the people will listen to you?" asked Zipporah.

But Moses wasn't sure.

Then Moses said, "Make me new sandals. The people will listen if I have new sandals."

So Zipporah made sandals for Moses of smooth leather fastened with thin sturdy strips. They were the finest sandals she had ever made.

"Here are your new sandals. Now do you think the people will listen to you?" asked Zipporah. But Moses wasn't sure.

Then Moses said, "Make me a new hat. The people will listen if I have a new hat."

So Zipporah made Moses a hat of the finest animal skins, cutting and measuring so that it would be a very good fit. It was the finest hat she had ever made.

"Here's your new hat. *Now* do you think the people will listen to you?" asked Zipporah.

But Moses wasn't sure.

Moses said, "Help me cut my beard. The people will listen if I cut my beard."

So Zipporah helped Moses cut his beard. She trimmed and clipped it oh so carefully, fixing it in a very stylish way. It was the finest trim she had ever given. By this time, Zipporah was getting a little bit weary of making things.

"All right, Moses," she said, still wanting to be helpful, "a new coat, new sandals, new hat and a newly trimmed beard. Will the people listen to you now?"

Moses thought for a moment and replied, "All these new things don't help. How can I stop worrying and just believe the people will listen."

Suddenly Zipporah had an idea. She told Moses. "Stay put and I'll be right back." In a few minutes she returned holding something in her hand.

"Moses, remember when God called you to do this job?"

"Yes," said Moses rather slowly.

"You told me that God promised to make you a great leader."

"Yes," said Moses, slowly again.

"And you said that God gave you a sign of that promise. Here is that sign, your walking stick." Moses looked surprised. Zipporah handed him the stick. Moses smiled and clutched the walking stick close to his chest, remembering God's promise.

"Oh, yes, I remember now. How could I forget. God promised to bless my faithful walking stick. God said I would use it to perform miracles so the Israelites would believe."

As Moses continued holding the stick closely, he breathed a prayer of thanksgiving. Zipporah looked on with happiness, too, grateful that Moses had remembered God's promise.

And grateful that Moses would stop asking her to make things.

Prayer

Heavenly Parent, help us remember when we forget how much you love us, when we forget that you are with us, everyday. *Amen.*

Thank the children for joining you and invite them to return to their seats.

Exodus 6:28–11:10

When the king saw that the frogs were dead, he became stubborn again and, just as the Lord had said, the king would not listen to Moses and Aaron.
(Exodus 8:15, *Today's English Version*)

Summary
In this reading from the book of Exodus, God sends the plagues to convince the king of Egypt to obey Moses. In today's homily, children participate in telling today's story through choral response.

Materials
Bible
poster board or newsprint
3 colored markers
easel
pointer or ruler

Before the homily, copy the choral reading of today's homily on poster board, using a different color for each voice (*king, Moses and narrator*).

Homily
Invite the children to come forward for today's homily and sit in a semicircle in front of you.

Be certain all children can see the poster.

Say to the children,
- What is a *promise*?
- Yes, a promise is a statement that we will do something for sure, no matter what.

- Today's story from the Bible is about a very mean, stubborn king who did not keep his promise.
- Over and over again, the king breaks his promise to Moses and the people of Israel.

Hold your Bible open to the book of Exodus as you tell today's story:

Over and over and over, Moses asked the king, "Please let my people go."

But the king would not!

Each time Moses asked and the king said no, a very annoying thing would happen to the king and to all the people in his land. The king would become afraid. He would say, "All right, you can go now."

But as soon as the annoying thing was over, he would change his mind.

Say to the children:
- Help me tell the story with this choral reading.

Note: Choose one child of reading age to be the *king*. Remaining children will together be the *narrator*. You or a child can be *Moses*. Point to the words as you read through the choral reading, helping the children with their parts as needed. Children that cannot read will be able to join in as they become familiar with the story's pattern. Use great expression on the italicized words.

King:
>Red water here,
>red water there,
>red water flowing everywhere.
>Moses, Moses,
>stop the red water!

Moses:
>Then let my people go!

Narrator (children):
>The king *said* he would.
>He *promised* he would.
>The king said, *"It's a deal, Moses."*
>But as soon as the red water went away,
>the king said *no!*

King:
>Green frogs here,
>green frogs there,
>green frogs jumping everywhere.
>Moses, Moses,
>stop the jumping green frogs.

Moses:
>Then let my people go!

Narrator (children):
>The king *said* he would.
>He *promised* he would.
>The king said, *"It's a deal, Moses."*
>But as soon as the frogs went away,
>the king said *no!*

King:
>Gray flies here,
>gray flies there,
>gray flies buzzing everywhere.
>Moses, Moses,
>stop the buzzing gray flies.

Moses:
>Then let my people go!

Narrator (children):
>The king *said* he would.
>He *promised* he would.
>The king said, *"It's a deal, Moses."*
>But as soon as the flies went away,
>the king said *no!*

King: Yellow gnats here,
>yellow gnats there,
>yellow gnats flying everywhere.
>Moses, Moses,
>stop the flying yellow gnats.

Moses:
>Then let my people go!

Narrator (children):
>The king *said* he would.
>He *promised* he would.
>The king said, *"It's a deal, Moses."*
>But as soon as the gnats went away,
>the king said *no!*

King:
> Grasshoppers here,
> grasshoppers there,
> hopping grasshoppers everywhere.
> Moses, Moses, stop the hopping grasshoppers.

Moses:
> Then let my people go!

Narrator (children):
> The king *said* he would.
> He *promised* he would.
> The king said, *"It's a deal, Moses."*
> But as soon as the grasshoppers went away,
> the king said *no!*

And so bad things happened to the king and all his people. Each time a new problem came to his people and his land he would promise to let the Israelites go. As soon as that problem went away, he would go back on his word. He would break his promise.

Say to the children:
- What do you think: will Moses and the people trust that the king will do what he says?
- What happens when we don't keep our promises?
- Why should we keep our promises?

Prayer

Dear God, you remind us that promises are important. We want to keep our promises. Please help us. *Amen.*

Thank the children for joining you and invite them to return to their seats.

Exodus 12:1-28

"When your children ask you, 'What does this ritual mean?' you will answer, 'It is the sacrifice of Passover to honor the Lord...'" (Exodus 12:26-27a, Today's English Version)

Summary

In today's reading from the book of Exodus, the Hebrews plan for Passover and their escape from slavery in Egypt. In today's homily, children discuss the meaning of celebrations and listen to today's story.

Materials

Bible
birthday party hat
Christmas stocking
small pumpkin
matzo bread or Seder plate

Note: Pictures of the above items may be substituted for the actual items.

Homily

Invite the children to come forward and sit in a semicircle around you.

Say to the children:
- What is a *celebration*?
- I brought some items that we use in celebrations. Who will help me?

Choose children to hold the birthday party hat, the pumpkin and the Christmas stocking, explaining that you will ask for their help when it is time. Continue:
- Birthdays are celebrations. Of the objects I brought today, which one would help us celebrate a birthday? *(Have children identify which object, then ask the child holding the birthday hat to hold it up high for everyone to see.)*
  — What do we do at birthday parties?
  — What does a birthday party mean?
- Christmas is a celebration. Which object helps us celebrate Christmas? *(Ask the child holding the Christmas stocking to hold it up high for everyone to see.)*
  — What does Christmas mean?
- Thanksgiving is a celebration. Which object would we use to help celebrate Thanksgiving? *(Ask the child holding the pumpkin to hold it up high for everyone to see.)*
  — What do we do at Thanksgiving?
  — What does Thanksgiving mean?

Collect the items and place them where children can see them. Continue:
- Today our Bible story is about a celebration that started a very long time ago.
- This celebration is called the Passover.
- Jews today still celebrate the Passover just as we celebrate the birth of Jesus at Christmas.
- Listen now as I tell the story of the Passover celebration.

Hold your Bible open to the book of Exodus as you tell today's story:

God said to Moses and his brother Aaron, "I am going to free you from the mean king and you shall no longer be their slaves. The Angel of Death will go throughout the land of Egypt. People will get sick and die. You must protect yourself and your families."

"All right, Lord, what should we do?" asked Aaron hurriedly. Both Moses and Aaron listened closely to the instructions of God.

God said, "Tell every family to prepare a special meal on the fourteenth day of this month. Each family will serve roasted meat, but not more than that family will eat. Serve the meat with herbs and a special bread."

"What if there is meat left over?" asked Moses. "What should we do with it?"

God said, "Burn it in the cooking fire."

Aaron looked very puzzled and said, "But God, I don't understand why we have to do that. Can't we leave it on the ground for the animals to eat?"

God said gently to Aaron, "You won't always understand my ways, Aaron. You are a human, not God."

Reluctantly, Aaron agreed.

Then Moses added, "God, what did you say about the sandals and the jewelry?

God replied, "Take with you the gold and silver jewelry that the Egyptians have given to you. Wear your sandals during and after the meal and don't take them off your feet so that when it is time to go, you will be ready."

"How will the destruction pass by *us* on that night?" asked Aaron.

"By the marks on the door...the marks that you shall put there before your meal," answered God. "You are my chosen people and you are marked as mine. Death will pass over you that night."

God continued instructing Moses and Aaron. "This is important," continued God. "I want your children and their children and all the people who live after you to know that you have been delivered from the mean stubborn king. You will celebrate every year and you will call the celebration *Passover*, because death *passed over* you."

Moses and Aaron began to tell the people the plan for their escape.

And so it happened as it was told.

Ask the children:
- What does *Passover* mean?

Show the matzo bread as a symbol of the Passover. You could give each child a piece to eat.

Conclude the homily by asking:
- Why do we have celebrations?
- What are *our* favorite celebrations?

Prayer

God, we celebrate to remember—to remember your goodness to your people through all ages. Help us to celebrate you today at church by remembering your love for us. *Amen.*

Thank the children for joining you and invite them to return to their seats.

Exodus 13:17-22

During the night he went in front of them in a pillar of fire to give them light so that they could travel night and day. (Exodus 13:21b, *Today's English Version*)

Summary

In this reading from the book of Exodus, God leads the Hebrews out of Egypt and guides them with a pillar of cloud and pillar of fire. In today's homily, the children recall things experienced by the senses and hear today's story.

Materials

Bible

Homily

Invite the children to come forward for today's homily and sit in a semicircle in front of you.

Say to the children:
- When we experience something, sometimes we can see it (*point to your eyes, have the children do so also*); sometimes we may be able to hear it (*point to ears*); sometimes we taste it (*mouth*); sometimes we feel it (*skin*); and sometimes we smell it (*nose*).
- What things do we *see* in our church? What things can we *hear*? Are there things we *taste*? And are there things we *feel*? Are there things we can *smell*?
- Today's story is about a young Hebrew girl who left Egypt with her family. She was just about your age. Her name is Leah. She experienced many things the night she and her family left Egypt.

Hold your Bible open to the book of Exodus as you tell today's story:

Mother said, "Hurry, Leah, get up! We must hurry." Mother shook me gently as I lay in bed.

"Why," I said, rubbing my sleepy eyes. "It is so dark outside. I don't want to leave. Let me stay here to sleep."

Mother reminded me that the evil king would harm us and keep us as slaves forever if we did not escape. So I reluctantly got up.

"Look, I guess I am ready! My sandals are still on my feet," I said, as I sat up on the warm cot where I had been sleeping.

A few minutes later I left our home with my mother, father and three brothers. We traveled into the dark, dark night with hundreds and hundreds of other people. Babies cried. Donkeys brayed. Men and women spoke in low,

hushed tones. A soft breeze blew through the cool of the desert night. But it didn't seem as dark as I thought it would on a night where there was no moon. Something strange was lighting the sky.

"Mother, what is that light?" I asked excitedly.

But mother didn't answer right away. Mother walked in a hurry. She held my hand tightly as she pulled me along, trying to hold on to me and carry my baby brother in her other arm.

"Come along now, Leah, and don't ask too many questions. God has come to rescue us from the cruel king."

"But I want to know about the light I see. Please tell me what it is!"

"Leah, I see your older brother Jonathan right ahead of us. I'll let him explain it to you. But you must continue to hurry along. For goodness sake, don't slow down."

So I caught up with my older brother Jonathan and held his hand as we walked through the night. This is what he told me:

"God is helping us get away from Egypt. Our people have been slaves for almost 400 years. God decided enough is enough. Other people say our leader Moses is up ahead, where you see the light in the sky. I'm not sure, but the light must be God. What do you think it is, Leah?"

"Oh," I said, "it looks like the top of a fire, but I can't really see any flames. It seems tall like a thick post or a pillar from a building. Lift me up on your shoulders, Jonathan, so I can see it better."

Jonathan did, but I still wasn't high enough to see it all. I was sure that Jonathan must know about the light. Jonathan was sixteen and I was only eight. He must know twice as much about God, I thought, as I gently rocked sitting on his shoulders. Pretty soon I felt myself getting very sleepy.

Say to the children:
- ■ Leah experienced many things that night in her escape from Egypt.
   — What did she see?
   — What did she hear?
   — What did she feel?

Prayer

Thank you, Creator God, for creating us with all our senses so we can experience many things. *Amen.*

Thank the children for joining you and invite them to return to their seats.

Exodus 13:17-22

During the day the Lord went in front of them in a pillar of cloud to show them the way, and during the night he went in front of them in a pillar of fire to give them light, so that they could travel night and day. (Exodus 13:21, *Today's English Version*)

Summary

In this reading from the book of Exodus, God leads the escaping Israelites with a pillar of fire. In today's homily, children experience a candle and incense, hear today's story and sing new words to a familiar children's song.

Materials

Bible
poster board 26" x 18"
2 colored markers
candle
incense in a burner
matches

Before the homily, print the words of the song from today's homily on poster board using one color marker for the chorus and a different color marker for the verse. Practice the song several times.

Homily

Invite the children to come forward for today's homily and sit in a semi-circle in front of you.

Say to the children:
- A symbol is an object or a drawing that has special meaning.
- Our church has many symbols. Today we will talk about two of them: incense and candles.

Light both the incense and the candle while the children watch. Continue:
- The light of the candle means many things…hope, love, God.
- The incense rises upward like our prayers going to God. Incense creates a sweet smell that reminds of the sweetness of Jesus.
- Listen to this story that happened a very long time ago. This story reminds me of our two church symbols.

Let the incense and candle continue to burn as you continue. Hold your Bible open to the book of Exodus as you tell today's story:

When the Hebrew people escaped from Egypt, Moses prayed to God. "Lord, how shall we know the way? We might get lost."

God said, "Trust me, Moses. I will not take you from the land of

Egypt only to have you get lost. I made the king let you go, didn't I? Then surely I can guide you in the desert."

So the hundreds and hundreds of people began their journey into the desert. "Oh, my, oh my," exclaimed the people. "What shall we do for light?" In their fear, some made torches from blankets. Some lit candles.

"Where is your faith?" said Moses. Aaron, his brother, said, "Yes, all of you need to trust in the God of our fathers, Abraham, Isaac and Jacob."

"We have to see," yelled the people. "What are we to do?"

"Trust God," said Moses.

But the people continued making small lights as they traveled. Their torches and candles blew out in the wind. The night grew darker and darker. Finally, when the last candle burned out and the last torch lost its glow...there it was! In the sky, a bright light that seem to reach like a flame from the heavens to the earth.

"Just as God promised," said Moses.

"I knew God would guide us," said Aaron. And the people looked into the sky at the pillar of fire, thankful once again, singing praises to the God of Abraham, Isaac and Jacob.

Say to the children:
- Let's learn a song to help us remember this wonderful story.

Using the tune "Twinkle, Twinkle Little Star," teach children the chorus of the song. Practice their part with them. Explain that you will motion with your hand when it is their turn to sing. You (or another adult volunteer) can sing the verses.

Chorus:
  Cloud by day, fire by night,
  God gave these to the Israelites!

Verse:
  Moses said go pack your tents;
  That's what they did and away they went.

Chorus

Verse:
  A woman said, "Where do we go?"
  Moses said, "We will know."

Chorus

Verse:
  One man said, "We're afraid!"
  Aaron said, "We've got it made!"

Chorus

If you wish, discuss with the children:
- Does our candle remind you of something in the story?
- What does our incense remind you of?

Prayer

Dear God, we are thankful for the sweet smells and the warm light that are in our church and in our worship. In the day and in the night, please guide us safely. *Amen.*

Thank the children for joining you and invite them to return to their seats.

Exodus 14:10-14, 21-25;15:20-21

The Israelites went through the sea on dry ground, with walls of water on both sides. (Exodus 14:22. *Today's English Version*)

Summary

In today's reading from the book of Exodus, God parts the Red Sea and saves the Israelites from the Egyptians. In today's homily, children listen to a creative retelling of this story.

Materials

Bible

Homily

Invite the children to come forward for today's homily and sit in a semi-circle in front of you. Hold your Bible open to the book of Exodus as you tell today's story:

"Grandpa, Grandpa, tell us a story," chimed the twins together. Grandpa was the best storyteller. They loved his stories about the old days.

"Oh, well, I suppose," he said reluctantly, with a twinkle in his eye. He always *acted* like he didn't want to tell stories, but they knew differently. He loved telling stories as much as they loved listening

"Grandpa, tell us the one about the great wall of water?" said Eli.

"Get comfortable, then," Grandfather said as they scrambled into his lap. And once again he began the familiar story about his boyhood as a Hebrew child.

"Once, long ago, the king of Egypt ruled the land. We were slaves. Our great leader Moses finally convinced the king to set us free. So we left the land of Egypt and traveled into the dark night."

"Grandpa," said Esau hurriedly, "Don't forget the part about the light!"

Grandpa didn't: "There was a big pillar of light far ahead of us. I remember my father saying, 'Son, that is the light of God leading us away from the cruel king.' In the day, instead of light, a huge cloud guided us. After traveling several days we camped close to the Red Sea."

Excitedly, Eli interrupted: "Grandpa, don't forget the part about the walls of water!"

Grandpa didn't: "The king changed his mind and wanted us to return to his land and be slaves. All his soldiers came after us and there was no place to go except straight into the water!

"My father and all the other Hebrew people said, 'Now what will we do?'

"Moses stood in front of us and held out his walking stick. Then *(use a hushed voice)* we heard the sound of a mighty wind, the water began to move *(move your hands in a churning motion).* The wind blew and blew and blew. Right before our eyes the water separated, rising like walls to form a road right across the sea. It grew higher and higher. *(Use arms and hands to express size and height.)* No one had *ever* seen such a thing as this."

"Grandpa, Grandpa, tell us the next part. I like it best!" said Eli.

Grandpa did: "The wind blew and that rushing water stood *straight up* on either side. When Moses said to walk, we did. We walked across the bottom of the sea with those huge walls of water on either side of us."

"Don't forget the part about the ground, Grandpa!" said Esau.

Grandpa didn't: "The most amazing thing anyone had ever seen—the ground was dry, bone dry! We all walked across the sea on dry ground, safely to the other side."

"Were you scared, Grandpa?" asked Eli.

"Oh yes, I was scared," replied Grandpa. "All the people were scared looking up at those big walls of water. But we listened to Moses our leader and trusted God. We believed God would protect us from the evil king, even if God had to spread the Red Sea apart to do it."

Say to the children:
- Grandpa said all the people were scared. What were they afraid of?
- What do you think they did when they were scared?
- Do we ever feel scared?
- What do *we* do when we feel scared?
- Can we still trust God even when we are scared?

Prayer

God, help us—like Moses and the people of Israel—to trust you when we are scared. *Amen.*

Thank the children for joining you and invite them to return to their seats.

Exodus 32:1-14

So all the people took off their gold earrings and brought them to Aaron. (Exodus 32:3, Today's English Version)

Summary

In today's reading from the book of Exodus, Aaron and the Hebrew people create and worship a gold idol. In today's homily, children discuss the nature of idols, then hear today's story.

Materials

Bible
bouquet of plastic or silk flowers
bouquet of fresh-cut flowers or a live, flowering plant
several pieces of gold jewelry

Homily

Invite the children to come forward for today's homily and sit in a semicircle in front of you.

Show children the gold jewelry and ask:
- Do you think that this gold jewelry is God?
- Why is this jewelry not God?

Let children examine the artificial bouquet and the real flowers. Discuss:
- How are these flowers alike? different?
- What do we miss with the fake flowers? *(smell, growth, life, insects, etc.)*
- The plastic (or silk) flowers are an imitation of the real, growing flowers. An imitation isn't the real thing.
- Today's story is about the Hebrew people making an imitation god from gold jewelry. *(Show the jewelry again.)* An imitation god is called an *idol*.
- Let's see what happens.

Hold your Bible open to the book of Exodus as you tell today's story:

The Hebrew people lived in the desert. They had not been happy with the food. They had not been happy with the water. They had not been happy with Moses or with God.

One day Moses said to his brother Aaron, "I must go up the mountain to talk with God. God will give us directions so we can leave this desert. Then we will know how to better worship God."

Aaron quickly said, "Who will be in charge of the people while you are gone?"

Moses replied, "You are to be boss until I get back. And don't forget Aaron, you must not make any idols to worship. Idols are imitations of the true God. Don't forget Aaron, we worship only the one, true God."

Moses went up the mountain. He was gone for a very, very long time. The people waited. They waited and waited and waited. It seemed like *too long* to wait. They became restless, waiting for Moses to return with God's directions.

Aaron tried to calm the people: "I know we have waited a long time, but we *must* wait for Moses. Moses will bring back directions from God."

So the people waited. They waited and waited and waited. It seemed like *too long* to wait. They became restless, waiting for Moses.

"We are sick and tired of all this waiting," moaned the people again. "When will Moses return?"

Aaron got tired of the people complaining and he, too, got tired of waiting for his brother. It seemed too long to wait. "All right," said Aaron. "Bring me all your jewelry, your gold earrings and necklaces, and put them into this big pot. We will start a fire under the pot and melt the gold. Then we can make a god to worship, *just* while we are waiting for Moses."

So the people ran to their tents, found all their jewelry and took it to Aaron. After it was melted they took the melted gold and made a god that looked like a cow.

Aaron watched as they danced around the golden idol that looked like a cow. Aaron knew it was wrong, he remembered what Moses had told him, but he just got tired of hearing the people complain so much. He worried what would happen when Moses came down from the mountain.

What do *you* think will happen when Moses returns?

Invite answers to this final question.

Prayer

Thank you, God, for being the true and real God. We know we must worship only you. *Amen.*

> Thank the children for joining you and invite them to return to their seats.

74

Numbers 11

He assembled seventy of the leaders and placed them around the Tent. (Numbers 11:24b, *Today's English Version*)

Summary

In this reading from Numbers, God tells Moses to choose seventy people to help him lead. In today's homily, children first help make a big job manageable, then listen to today's story.

Materials

Bible
plastic container containing 1 cup uncooked elbow macaroni

Homily

Invite the children to come forward for today's homily and sit in a semicircle in front of you.

Begin the homily by discussing:
- What are some big jobs you have to do around your house?
- Sometimes jobs are too big for one person.

Dump the macaroni on the floor in front of the children. Spread it out with your hand. Continue:
- This would take one person a long time to clean up. But if several of us pick up, it won't take us long at all.
- Will you help me pick up the macaroni?

Together pick up the spilled macaroni, then say:
- Today's story is about one person needing help with a big job.

Hold your Bible open to the book of Numbers as you tell today's story:

The Hebrew people had been living in the desert for a long time. They were very tired of eating the same food day after day. The people complained and whined to Moses, their leader.

One day Zipporah, the wife of Moses, was busy cooking little cakes from the crushed seeds called manna: yes, manna—*the food everyone was tired of eating.*

Moses said in an angry voice. "What am I supposed to do, Zipporah? The people are whining. All they do is complain."

Zipporah stopped cooking and went to his side. "Here, Moses, let's have a cool drink while we think about what to do!"

Moses held the cups while Zipporah poured them each a drink of fresh water.

In the quiet of the moment Moses heard God speak to him: "Moses, I see that you are weary and tired. Gather seventy good men and bring them to the…"

"But God," Moses interrupted, "how will that help? What good will *that* do?"

"Moses, I know you are tired of hearing the complaints of the people. I want you…"

Moses interrupted God again: "But God, these people don't listen." Zipporah nodded in agreement.

Once again God said, "Moses, I see that you are weary and tired, so gather seventy good men. Bring them to the door…"

And yet again, before God could finish, Moses interrupted: "But, God…"

This time God spoke firmly to Moses: "Moses, now *you* are not listening! You are tired of the people complaining. Now I need *you* to stop complaining and listen to what I am trying to say to *you*."

Zipporah nudged Moses and whispered, "You better listen now, Moses."

God said, "Gather seventy friends to share the burden of leading the people. *Then it won't be so hard for you, Moses*. Then you won't carry the responsibility alone."

So Moses did as God asked. He gathered seventy friends and asked for their help. They understood and began to praise God.

Zipporah said, "Look Moses, your friends are happy to share the job of leading the people." Moses agreed. Moses felt relieved. Now his job wouldn't be so hard.

If you wish, discuss with the children:
- When I spilled the macaroni we had a big job to pick them up. What big job did Moses have to do?
- How did God help Moses and Zipporah?

Prayer

Thank you, God, for letting us share jobs so they don't seem so big. Thank you for this story about Moses. *Amen.*

Thank the children for joining you and invite them to return to their seats.

Numbers 11:31-35

Suddenly the Lord sent a wind that brought quails from the sea, flying three feet above the ground. (Numbers 11:31a, *Today's English Version*)

Summary
In today's reading from Numbers, God sends quail for food to the Hebrew people. In today's homily, children listen to a creative retelling of this story.

Materials
Bible
4 pieces of white 8" x 11" poster board
colored felt markers

Before the homily prepare simple drawings of a sun, yellow seeds, gray billowing clouds and gray birds, one on each poster board.

Homily
Invite the children to come forward for today's homily and sit in a semi-circle in front of you.

Say to the children:
- What is a job or chore that you have to do every day? *(Allow for several responses.)*
- Do you ever get tired of doing these jobs or chores? Why?
- Today's story is about a young boy named Samuel who had to gather seeds every morning.

Hold your Bible open to the book of Numbers as you tell today's story:

Every morning we get up early *(show picture of sun)*. Mother says to us, "Come along now, children…you, too, Samuel. Don't be slow! We have to gather the manna while it is early."

So off we go. I'm usually stumbling and grumbling with the big cloth bag slung over my shoulder, rushing with my family toward the desert.

"Wait for me!" I yell to my cousins. The hardest part is getting up early. Once we reach the desert, gathering manna is always fun.

I didn't know what manna was at first, but I do know I am very tired of eating it.

David, my cousin, explained, "Manna is special food from God. After our people left Egypt and all the food ran out, God gave us manna, the yellow seeds. *(Hold up the picture of the yellow seeds.)* We grind the manna to make bread."

David tells the story many times, or at least as often as we want to hear it. He loves the story too.

Every day is much the same: Get up. Gather manna in our bags.

Return home. And mostly it is always sunny. Day after day, always the same.

Today, like always, we are up early. "Wait for me!" I yell like I always do.

We arrive at a place in the desert where seeds are on the ground. Soon my bag is heavy and half-full. Mostly I look down toward the ground when I work. Manna—I'm so tired of manna.

"Look up!" yells David, suddenly. "There!" He points straight ahead. We all drop our bags.

Shading my eyes from the bright morning sun, I squint hard as the wind blows in my face.

Straight ahead it looks like a large gray cloud very close to the ground. It seems to be moving closer. *(Hold up picture of clouds.)*

"What is it?" I ask excitedly. No one is sure yet. By now, all the adults stop working to look.

"What is it?" I ask again. Still no one is sure. But we are sure of one thing: it is moving closer and it is very low to the ground.

"Perhaps it is a huge dust storm," says one of the neighbor women.

"Could it be the Egyptians riding horseback to capture us again?" asks an older man.

The adults try to guess. So do the children. "It looks like big gray pillows being thrown through the air by the sky giants," cries my younger sister. She doesn't know. No one knows.

Soon one of the men calls to everyone, "I see wings!"

"So do I," yells David.

I see wings, too.

We all stand still. We all strain hard to see. We all stare in surprise as birds appear—hundreds and hundreds of them. *(Hold up picture of birds.)* The birds begin to land.

Uncle Joseph says, "Praise God," really loudly. Other people join him.

We sing. We dance. We run back and forth among the birds as the adults begin catching them.

Mother says to her friends, "At last, we can have something to eat besides manna." Everyone is *so* tired of eating manna, especially me. Uncle Joseph keeps saying, "Praise God."

We all gather our things and head home excitedly. We will have something to eat besides manna. My cousins and I run all the way home.

Prayer

Thank you, God, for the special stories of our faith. Thank you this story that reminds us how you provided for your people. Thank you for all the good things you give *us* to eat. *Amen.*

Thank the children for joining you and invite them to return to their seats.

Numbers 22:1-40

"What have I done to you? Why have you beaten me these three times?" (Numbers 22:28b, Today's English Version)

Summary

In this reading from the book of Numbers, God gets Balaam's attention through his donkey. In today's homily, the children first discuss figuring out problems, then listen to today's story.

Materials

Bible
donkey drawing, found on page 81

Homily

Invite the children to come forward for today's homily. Ask them to sit in a semicircle in front of you.

Say to the children:
- Imagine that your friend Suzie has a bump on her head. What might have happened?
- Imagine that you walk into your kitchen and the floor is all sticky. What might have happened?
- Imagine you are riding your faithful donkey when suddenly he stops and runs off the road into a field. What might have happened?
- Today's story is about a man and his donkey. Let's listen as the donkey tells the story.

Hold your Bible open to the book of Numbers as you tell today's story:

My name is Japhed. I am an old donkey. *(Display the donkey picture.)* I like to sleep in hay. I like to stand out in the warm sun.

Let me tell you a story about my younger days.

Once a mean king was afraid of the Hebrew people. He sent messengers to ask my owner Balaam to help.

The messengers said, "Balaam, look at all the Hebrews that are camped near us. They will overtake us and destroy our people. Please help us."

Balaam said, "First, I have to ask God what to do."

God told Balaam, "Don't go to the cruel king. The Hebrews are my special people."

Balaam told the king's men, "No."

The messengers took the message back to the king. So the king sent his best leaders to convince Balaam.

But Balaam trusted God and said, "Even if the king gives me lots of money, I won't do it."

I know this all happened because I was outside munching on hay and I heard them talking. Eventually they *did* convince Balaam to go talk with the king.

Next morning Balaam said, "All right, Japhed, it's time to go. We have a long trip ahead."

And off we went down a road I knew very well.

Then a strange thing happened: I saw something Balaam didn't see. I saw an angel with a big sword right in the middle of the road. I left that road in a hurry, and headed straight for the field.

Balaam said, "Japhed, don't turn." But I did. Balaam took a stick, hit my backside and pulled me back to the road. He said, "All right, Japhed, it is time to go."

We only went a little ways and there stood that angel, right in the middle of the road again. I left the road and went into the field.

Balaam said, "Japhed, don't turn!" Balaam took a stick and hit my backside again and then pulled me back to the road.

He said, "All right, Japhed, that's enough. It is time to go."

We only went a little ways and there was that same angel. Can you guess where the angel was standing?

Yes, right in the middle of the road! I knew what would happen if I ran into the field. Instead I went to my knees and lay stiff as a board!

Balaam said, "Japhed, get up!" And he hit my backside with the stick. And again he said, "Japhed, get up!" I still didn't move. Then he hit my backside more. He did not see the angel in the middle of the road *like I did*.

Finally I spoke to Balaam and said, "Haven't I been a good donkey?"

Balaam's mouth dropped open. He'd never heard a donkey speak before.

"Have I ever taken you down a wrong path?" I asked.

Balaam just stared.

"Well?"

Finally, softy, Balaam said, "No." Balaam said he was sorry. Then Balaam looked up and saw the angel standing in the road—a little late for my backside, perhaps, but he got the point.

Those were days long ago, but Balaam's always remembered how important it is to listen to God… and to think things through instead of reaching for a stick.

I like that.

Prayer

Thank you, God, for the story of Balaam and his donkey. Help us, like Balaam, to learn to listen to you. *Amen.*

Thank the children for joining you and invite them to return to their seats.

Numbers 27:12-23

The Lord said to Moses, "Take Joshua son of Nun, a capable man, and place your hands on his head." (Numbers 27:18, *Today's English Version*)

Summary

In today's reading from the book of Numbers, God tells Moses to make Joshua the new leader for the people of Israel. In today's homily, children first pretend to be hiking, then listen to today's story.

Materials

Bible
backpack containing:
  hat
  windbreaker or jacket
  flashlight
  jingle bells
  walking stick

Before the homily memorize the opening "hike" portion of the homily so you won't have to read it.

Homily

Invite the children to come forward for today's homily and sit in a semi-circle in front of you.

Begin the homily by removing the hat and jacket from the backpack and putting them on. Put on the backpack, lift your walking stick, stand up and say to the children:
- Let's pretend that we are going on a hike today.
- Stand up with me and let's get started!

Begin walking in place, slowly and deliberately. The children will follow.
- I am your leader so follow me.
- Here comes a mountain. We will have to climb harder now. Up! Up! Up! Whew.
- Now we need to go down. Careful, don't fall. Watch out for the rocks and the stones.
- Good, now we are down the mountain. Let's stop and have a drink. *(Pretend to drink.)*
- Time to move on. Oh, watch out there are some low branches ahead. *(Duck your head.)* Don't get hit.
- Oh no, be very quiet! Hold still! There's a large snake ahead. *(Pause.)* Whew, good thing we were quiet; the snake slithered away.
- Here's a big ditch. Step carefully over it. *(Take a large step.)*
- Let's make sure we let the bears know we are coming. *(Jingle the bells.)*
- It's getting late. The sun has gone down. *(Turn on the flashlight.)* We better head home and rest.

Invite children to be seated. Discuss:
- I was your leader on our hike. What did I do as the leader?
- If one of you were going to be the leader of our pretend hike, what will you need to know to be a good leader?
- Today's Bible story is about Moses, a leader of the Hebrew people.

Moses was a strong leader, a good leader, but a very tired leader. Let's see what happens.

Hold your Bible to the book of Numbers as you tell today's story:

Moses said to God, "Who should be the leader of the Hebrew people? I am getting old now and we need a new leader."

God said "Yes, Moses, your time for leading is almost over. Who do *you* think should take your place."

Moses thought for a moment and then said, "God, I know who might be a good leader. What about Hepher? Hepher has been a strong hunter for many years."

God stayed silent and then said thoughtfully, "No, Moses, Hepher is a good hunter, but I don't think he's the right leader for my people."

"Well, then, how about Gilead?" said Moses. "Gilead has been a gallant soldier and a wonderful father to his many children."

God stayed silent and then said thoughtfully, "No, Moses, Gilead is a gallant soldier and wonderful father, but I don't think he's the right leader for my people."

Moses thought and thought for a long time. Moses thought about all the persons who God might pick.

Finally he said, "How about Hannah. She's a gifted speaker and loved by all. She speaks so clearly."

And for the third time God stayed silent and then said thoughtfully, "No, Moses, Hannah is a gifted speaker and loved, but I don't think she's the right leader for my people."

"Well, God," said Moses, "I've run out of ideas. I don't know who would be a good leader. I just know we need someone who can lead our people, who can spot dangers up ahead and who will not let the people wander off the path."

Then God said, "I've thought of someone who is strong, gallant and good at speaking, Moses. Remember Joshua, the son of Nun?"

Moses remembered right away and said, "Yes, God, he is very capable."

God said, "Find Joshua and take him before the priest and all the people. Place your hand upon him, give him the leader's blessing and tell everyone Joshua will now be the new leader of the Hebrews."

So Moses did what God told him to do.

Prayer

God, thank you for giving *us* leaders that guide us and help us: for moms and dads, priests and pastors, teachers and grandparents. *Amen.*

Thank the children for joining you and invite them to return to their seats.

Deuteronomy 4:1-9

"Obey all the laws that I am
teaching you, and you will live..."
(Deuteronomy 4:1b,
Today's English Version)

Summary

In today's reading from the book of Deuteronomy, Moses gives God's people God's instructions. In today's homily, children first discuss rules and laws, then listen to today's story.

Materials

Bible
poster board
colored felt markers

Homily

Invite the children to come forward for today's homily and sit in a semi-circle in front of you.

Begin the homily by discussing:
- We have rules and laws that help us and protect us. Our city has rules. Our schools have rules. Our parents have rules.
- What is a rule your parents have given you? *(List a variety of responses on the poster board.)*
- There's a special word we use when we have followed a rule and done what the rule asked us to do. Do you know that word?

Write the word *obey* on the poster board. Ask the children to say the word with you. Continue:

- Sometimes we don't follow the rules. Which of the rules we mentioned are hard to follow? *(Circle those that children mention.)*
- What other rules are hard to follow? How about brushing your teeth before going to bed? hanging up your clothes? not hitting your brother or sister?
- There's another special word we use when we have *not* followed a rule. Do you know that word?

Write the word *disobey* on the poster board. Ask the children to say the word with you. Continue:

- We need to be reminded of rules because we forget.
- And that's what today's story is all about.

Hold your Bible open to the book of Deuteronomy as you tell today's story:

Moses gathered the people together. He climbed to the top of a tall rock so that all the people could see, and hear him.

Moses held up his hands to silence the crowd.

He said, "God, the true God, wants you to obey God's rules." Some of the people did not pay attention when Moses was speaking.

So Moses said again, "God, the true God, wants you to obey God's rules."

Then one man said, "Moses, we are tired of rules. There are too many rules. Let's get rid of at least half of the rules."

But Moses quickly replied, "God says you must not get rid of *any* of the rules."

Then a woman in the crowd yelled out to Moses, "If the rules are good, then lets make up even *more* rules. God will like that, right?"

But Moses replied, "No, God says do not add anything to the rules that God has given you. Don't make up more rules."

Someone else said, "Moses do we have to obey every day. Can't we have a day off?"

Someone else said, "Let's pick the rules we like and forget the rest of them."

And the people grumbled, continuing to question Moses and suggesting changes.

Then Moses said, "If you obey the rules, other people will know how wise you are. They will know that you worship the true God."

Moses continued to remind the people of God's rules saying, "Don't forget! Be on your guard. Tell your children. Tell your grandchildren. Don't ever let anyone forget God's rules."

Prayer

Thank you, our Heavenly Parent, for giving us your rules, rules to keep us safe, rules to help us know you, rules to share your love. *Amen.*

Thank the children for joining you and invite them to return to their seats.

Deuteronomy 5:6-21

"I am the Lord your God, who rescued you from Egypt, where you were slaves." (Deuteronomy 5:6, Today's English Version)

Summary

In today's reading from the book of Deuteronomy, God gives the Hebrews the Ten Commandments. In today's homily, children first discuss people to whom they listen, then hear a creative retelling of today's story.

Materials

Bible

Homily

Invite the children to come forward for today's homily and sit in a semicircle in front of you.

Begin the homily by discussing:

- Whose voices do we hear everyday? Whose voices do you hear at home? at church? at school?
- Whose voices do we listen to most closely?
- Have you ever thought about what God's voice would sound like if God talked to us?
- How closely would we listen to God's voice, if we heard it today?
- That's what today's story is about. Let's listen and see what God has to say…and what God might sound like.

Hold your Bible open to the book of Deuteronomy as you tell today's story:

"Grandma, Grandma, please tell us the story about the dancing cow," cries my little brother Seth. He is only three and confuses things. So I say, "Seth, the *people* danced, not the cow!"

Grandma says, "That's all right; I know which story you love to hear."

And so she begins…just like she always does:

"I remember," says Grandmother, "that we were watching people dance around a big, golden cow—even though they weren't supposed to.

"The people yelled, 'We want God to tell us what to do! We are tired of waiting for Moses to come back from the mountain with God's commands.

"Suddenly the sky blackened. We thought it was a cloud. 'Papa,' I cried. 'Why is it so dark?' The dancing stopped; everyone stood *very* still. Smoke rose from the top of the mountain, blocking the sun.

"'Fire!' yelled some of the people.

"'Look!' someone else cried. 'Moses is walking from the smoke.

He's holding something big in his arms. He's coming down the mountain.'

"'Moses is bringing God's commandments,' Papa said hopefully.

"Well, children, the people around the cow were confused; some ran away from the mountain, some hid from the sight of the fire, and some started dancing again.

"And just then, the thunder *cracked,* and lightening *flashed* through the sky. Wind blew. A drizzle of rain fell on my arm. It sent a cool chill up my spine.

"People screamed and yelled. I tried to see, but there were adults all around me, blocking my view.

"'Papa, what is it?' I said, jumping higher, trying to get a better look. 'What are people yelling about, Papa?'

"Papa didn't answer so I held his hand tightly, too afraid to look, yet too curious *not* to look.

"Soon people said 'Sh, sh, quiet!' Everyone got quiet. Even the thunder stopped.

"In a loud voice, Moses said: 'God spoke to me on the mountains. God said, "You shall have no other gods before me. I am the creator and you must only worship me."'

"Most of the people, including my father and me, fell to the ground in silence."

And then Seth interrupts Grandma and asks, "But Grandmother, what does God's voice sound like? Have *you* ever heard God's voice?"

"Hush, Seth," I say. "Let her finish the story!"

"Oh, child, that's all right," says Grandma, putting her arms around both of us. "The voice of God? Well, child, yes, I've heard it. It's strong like big waves on the sea, but gentle like a breeze through grass. It's loud like thunder, but soft like a mother's lullaby. It's frightening like the roar of a lion in the desert, yet as loving as the mewing of a tiny kitten. God's voice is…" Grandma's voice trails off.

"See, Seth, now we'll never hear the rest of the story!"

But neither of us mind, really. We've heard the story many times. And we both feel very safe and warm within Grandmother's arms. We close our eyes and imagine the voice of God, that strong, strange, gentle, scary, loving voice calling us to love God, to love each other, to do our best not to lie, cheat, steal or hurt.

I wonder what the voice of God sounds like?

If you wish, invite children to respond to this final question.

Prayer

Dear God, speak to us. Help us to hear your voice in the world around us and the people who love us. *Amen.*

Thank the children for joining you and invite them to return to their seats.

Joshua 4:1-24

"These stones will always remind the people of Israel of what happened here."
(Joshua 4:7b, *Today's English Version*)

Summary

In today's reading from the book of Joshua, Joshua builds a memorial to Israel's safe crossing of the Jordan River. In today's homily, children first discuss Israel's "Covenant Box," listen to today's story and learn a simple song.

Materials

Bible
2 sheets of poster boards
colored felt markers
ornate box or jewelry chest

Before the homily print on a sheet of poster board the words to the song found at the end of the homily.

Homily

Invite the children to come forward for today's homily and sit in a semicircle in front of you.

Explain:
- Long ago, the Hebrew people lived very differently from the way we do. They traveled by walking. They slept in tents.
- They also worshiped God in different ways, too. They did not worship in churches but in a big tent, and they put all their religious reminders and sacred objects in a box. *(Show children the box.)*
- Their box, however, was much larger than this. It was so large that it took several people to carry it. They called it a Covenant Box or Promise Box.
- Because this box held very special worship items, the priests would carry the Promise Box in front of the people when they walked.

Draw a wide blue river on a sheet of poster board, using two wavy lines several inches apart. Continue:
- When the people of Israel reached the Jordan River, they did not know how to get across the deep, dangerous water. *(Point to the lines, showing one side, then the other.)* They waited for Joshua, their leader, to direct them.

Hold your Bible open to the book of Joshua as you tell today's story:

"The water is deep! The river is wide!" cried the Hebrew people. "How can we get across the river?"

Joshua knew what they must do. First, he selected twelve men, one from each of the twelve tribes.

Then Joshua said to the priests, "Lift the Promise Box high and step into the water."

So the priests did as Joshua said. As the priests stepped into the water, the water suddenly stopped flowing! The river bottom began to dry!

Joshua said to the priests, "Stand right where you are! Keep the box high in the air until all the people have crossed over."

The people said, "We can walk across the river now!" And that's just what they did.

Then to the twelve men Joshua said, "As you walk across the dry river, I want each of you to pick up one large stone and carry it to the other side with you."

After all the people were across the river, Joshua told the priests with the Promise Box to cross. Then the twelve men stacked the large stones into a pile that might have looked like this. *(On the poster board, beside the river, draw a triangular stack using twelve black circles representing the twelve stones.)*

"These rocks will be a reminder to you and to your children," said Joshua, "that God provided a way for you to cross the river."

The people sang and worshiped God, praising God and saying, "Hallelujah!"

Say to the children:
- The Hebrew people sang and praised God.
- Let's do that too!

Place the poster board with the words of the song where it can be seen by both children and the parish members. Teach everyone—children and parish members alike—to sing the song and to do the accompanying motions. The tune is "Michael, Row the Boat Ashore."

1. The river is deep and the river is wide. *(Place hands parallel horizontally and then vertically.)*
Hallelujah! *(Clap four times in rhythm.)*
The river is deep and the river is wide. *(Place hands parallel horizontally and then vertically.)*
Hallelujah!
(Clap four times in rhythm.)

2. Take the box and hold it high. *(Lift arms up above head.)*
Hallelujah! *(Clap four times in rhythm.)*
Take the box and hold it high. *(Lift arms up above head.)*
Hallelujah! *(Clap four times in rhythm.)*

3. Walk on over to the other side. *(Hands move as feet, walking away from body.)*
Hallelujah! *(Clap four times in rhythm.)*
Walk on over to the other side. *(Hands move as feet, walking away from body.)*
Hallelujah! *(Clap four times in rhythm.)*

4. Keep God first in your life always. *(Cross arms over chest; lift index finger.)*
Hallelujah! *(Clap four times in rhythm.)*
Keep God first in your life always. *(Cross arms over chest; lift index finger.)*
Hallelujah! *(Clap four times in rhythm.)*

Prayer

Thank you, dear God, for helping your people. Thank you for helping us. *Amen.*

Thank the children for joining you and invite them to return to their seats.

Joshua 24:1-2a, 14-25

"As for my family and me, we will serve the Lord." (Joshua 24:15b, *Today's English Version*)

Summary

In today's reading from the book of Joshua, the people of Israel promise to serve God. In today's homily, children first discuss promise-making and promise-keeping, then make a promise and hear today's story.

Materials

Bible
1 sheet of poster board
easel
felt marker
1 large sheet of gray or brown construction paper
scissors

Before the homily, cut out a large rock shape from the gray or brown construction paper.

Homily

Invite the children to come forward for today's homily and sit in a semicircle in front of you.

To begin the homily, discuss:
- Have any of us been reminded to do something that we had promised we would do? *(Offer a personal example to help children get started.)*
- Who reminded you? How did they remind you?
- Let's make a promise, and then make a reminder to help us remember our promise.
- Let's promise to be quiet listeners during our story. Do you promise?

Write the promise on the poster board (for example, *We promise to be quiet listeners*). Then draw a simple picture to illustrate the promise (for example, an ear or a index finger raised to lips).

Continue:
- Let's use this poster as *our reminder* that we will listen today.
- During the story when you look up here *(point to the poster board)*, you will be reminded to listen.
- Today's Bible story is about Joshua and the Hebrew people. The people of Israel also promised to listen. And Joshua made them a reminder. Let's see if we can discover what that reminder was.

Hold your Bible open to the book of Joshua as you tell today's story:

Joshua called all the people together. They came from the east. They came from the west. They came from the north. They came from the south.

Many, many people gathered to hear their leader Joshua speak to them.

"You must love and worship only the true God," said Joshua. "Don't make any pretend gods from wood or stone. Don't make a gold cow like our people did long ago."

The crowd listened as Joshua spoke. Joshua was their leader.

Joshua said firmly, "My family and I will serve only the true God. But what about the rest of you?"

"We would never leave the true God to worship pretend gods," said all the people.

"Are you sure?" said Joshua. "How do you know you can trust God?"

One man yelled loudly, "We *can* trust God because our true God took us out of slavery! We won't make false gods because they are not real."

A woman then ran in front of the crowd shouting, "Yes, we *can* trust the true God. Our true God did miracles to help us. God helped us cross the Red Sea to escape from the wicked king."

"God fed us manna when there was no food," said a young boy. "Then God sent us quail when we grew tired of only manna!"

Someone else yelled, "God kept us safe as we traveled through the desert. God gave us light at night so we could find our way. We can always trust God."

Then Joshua said to the people, "But God wants you to do the right thing. Can you do that?"

"Yes, yes," cried the people loudly.

"All right, but I think you will need something to remind you that you have made this pledge and promise. I will write your promise on this stone so that you will always remember what we said here today."

And Joshua did just that. He took a smooth rock and wrote the words so that they would always remember. *(Write on the construction paper rock the words* We promise to do what is right*)*

"This stone will be a witness. This stone will be a reminder. This stone will help you remember that you have made a promise to worship the true God."

If you wish, discuss:
- What did the people of Israel promise?
- What reminder of the promise did Joshua create?
- Did we keep *our* promise to be quiet listeners?
- Did our reminder help?
- What reminders do we have here in our church? What things remind us to love God? to help others? to worship?

Prayer

Thank you, Heavenly Parent, for reminding us to love you, follow you and worship you. *Amen.*

Thank the children for joining you and invite them to return to their seats.

Judges 16:14-22

Delilah lulled Samson to sleep in her lap. (Judges 16:19a, *Today's English Version*)

Summary

In this reading from the book of Judges, Samson loses his strength when he yields to the persistent questioning of Delilah. In today's homily, children first discuss the challenge of saying no, then hear today's story and learn a simple song.

Materials

Bible
shiny quarter, new or polished
poster board
felt marker

Before the homily print on the sheet of poster board the words to the song found at the end of the homily.

Homily

Invite the children to come forward for today's homily and sit in a semicircle in front of you.

Make sure all the children can see the poster board on which you've printed the words of the song.

With the children, discuss:
- Let's pretend. Let's pretend you have a shiny new quarter, like this. *(Show quarter.)*
- Now pretend you accidentally leave your shiny new quarter out on the sidewalk in front of your house. *(Lay quarter on floor before the children.)* What do you think might happen to your quarter? *(Snatch the quarter away.)* That's right; someone will probably take your quarter.
- If you lost your quarter because you left it on the sidewalk, what do you think might happen if you left *another* quarter outside on the sidewalk the next day?
- Let's pretend you have another shiny new quarter. A friend says to you, "Hey, wouldn't it be fun to put your quarter out on the sidewalk?" Would you do it?
- Let's pretend your friend keeps begging you to leave your quarter on the sidewalk, over and over and over. Every time you see this friend, he or she asks you to leave your quarter out on the sidewalk.
- You really like your friend. You like doing things that make your friend happy. Do you do it? Do you leave your quarter on the sidewalk?
- Is it hard to say no when someone you like keeps asking, isn't it?
- Has something like this ever happened to you? It happened in today's Bible story. Let's listen.

Hold your Bible open to the book of Judges as you tell today's story:

God said, "Samson, I will give you special strength to be the leader of the Hebrews, but you must never cut your hair or your strength will leave you."

Samson was happy that God chose him. Samson always tried to do what would please God.

But sometimes Samson had trouble doing what he knew was right. It was especially hard for him when someone he liked asked him to do something wrong.

Samson liked Delilah, a beautiful woman who dressed in fancy clothes and wore gold jewelry. They spent lots of time together. But Delilah was really a spy for Samson's enemies. The enemies asked her to find out what made Samson strong.

"Samson, what makes you so strong?" Delilah asked.

But Samson didn't tell her the truth. He made up a silly answer because it was hard for him to just say no and mean it!

He told her, "If I am tied up with the string from my bow and arrows, then I will be as weak as anyone else."

Delilah waited until Samson was asleep and tied him with bow string. But when Samson awoke, he broke loose.

Again Delilah begged and nagged Samson to tell her the secret of his strength. So he told her, "If I am tied with new rope, then I will be as weak as anyone else."

Delilah waited until Samson was asleep and tied him with the new rope. But when Samson awoke, he broke loose.

Delilah kept asking.

Samson said, "If my long hair is wrapped around this wood, I won't be able to break loose."

Delilah waited until Samson was asleep and wrapped his long hair around the wood. But when Samson awoke, he broke loose.

Delilah asked over and over *and over* until Samson *finally* gave in and said, "If you cut my hair I will lose all my strength."

What do you think Delilah did? Yes, that's right, the next time Samson slept, she cut his hair. Then Samson was captured by his enemies.

Say to the children:
- When someone keeps asking us to do something, especially if we know things could turn out bad, what should we do?
- Let's learn a song to help us remember today's story.

Teach children this song, sung to the tune of "Twinkle, Twinkle, Little Star":

> God gave Samson lots of strength,
> But he did not stop to think.
> He was tricked,
> He was fooled,
> By Delilah with her jewels.
> God gave Samson lots of strength,
> But he did not stop to think!

Prayer

God, help us to think hard and say no when we someone urges us to do something we think is wrong. *Amen.*

Thank the children for joining you and invite them to return to their seats.

Ruth 1:1-17

But Ruth answered, "Don't ask me to leave you! Let me go with you. Wherever you go, I will go; wherever you live, I will live." (Ruth 1:16a, *Today's English Version*)

Summary

In this reading from the book of Ruth, Ruth pledges herself to her mother-in-law, Naomi. In today's homily, children discuss different kinds of families, then hear today's story.

Materials

Bible
pictures depicting a variety of families and family structures

Homily

Invite the children to come forward for today's homily and sit in a semicircle in front of you.

Begin the homilies by discussing:
- What is a *family*? *(Affirm all responses; share your own definition as well.)*
- Who are the people in *your* family?

Show the children the pictures of families. Explain:
- Families are people who live together and love each other.
- Here are pictures of different groups of people that can be families.

Discuss each picture briefly. Note that not all families are the same. Continue:
- Today's story is about a family. The story has some sad parts and some happy parts.
- The story begins in a town that we hear about every Christmas, the same town where Jesus was born, Bethlehem.
- But this story happened a long time before the Christmas story.

Hold your Bible open to the book of Ruth as you tell today's story:

Long ago in Bethlehem, a mom, dad and two sons lived. They liked living in Bethlehem, but because it was hard to get work and or find food, they decided to move to another country.

The country they moved to was Moab, a place very different from Bethlehem. Naomi, the mom, said to her family, "The people of Moab don't worship God like we do. But we need work and we need food. So this is where we will stay."

Not long after they were living in this new country of Moab, the dad

got very sick and died, leaving his wife, Naomi, and his two sons.

Naomi felt very, very sad. "I miss your dad so much," she told her sons. They missed their dad, too!

Naomi's sons were fine young men and soon each found a woman to marry. This made Naomi happy.

For ten years, the five of them lived together: Naomi, her two sons and their wives. They were busy being a family.

But then another sad thing happened. Naomi's two sons became ill and died. Naomi cried and cried. She said, "My heart feels broken and I feel angry. I have lost my dear husband, and now my two sons!"

In her sadness and grief, her two daughters-in-law, the wives of her two sons, stayed with her.

"We will stay with you, Naomi," they said. "We will comfort and care for you because you are sad, and because we love you."

They held Naomi as she cried. They listened with attention when Naomi talk about her sons.

Naomi's son's wives seemed like true daughters to her. They continued to stay with Naomi, help her and be a family.

But one day, Naomi heard Bethlehem once again had food and work. She was glad. Her heart rejoiced to think that she could return to her own country.

Naomi told the daughters-in-law, "I miss worshiping God like I used to. I want to go back to Bethlehem. You two should stay in your own country, find *new* husbands and make new families."

One of the daughters-in-law did stay in Moab, but the other one named Ruth had grown to love Naomi too much to leave her.

Ruth insisted, "Wherever you go, Naomi, I will go. I want to be with you, even if I have to leave my own country." She even wanted to worship God in the way that Naomi did.

And so the two of them, Naomi and Ruth, left Moab and moved to Bethlehem. They returned to Naomi's home.

If you wish, discuss with the children:
■ What parts of the story did you like best? *(If children do not respond, offer your own response to the story.)*
■ God gives all of us families…and people to love like family.

Prayer

Thank you, God, for love and for family. Thank you for all the people in our lives that love us and care for us. Thank you for the story of Naomi and Ruth. *Amen.*

Thank the children for joining you and invite them to return to their seats.